You've Got Ghosts!
Haunted Tales from the Inbox

Jennifer Lauer
and
Dave Schumacher

Schiffer Publishing Ltd
4880 Lower Valley Road Atglen, Pennsylvania 19310

Cover cartoon image by Derek Arneson and Troy Hartman
Text and images by authors unless otherwise noted
Ouija is a registered trademark of Parker Brothers.

Library of Congress Control Number: 2011933277

Designed by Bruce Waters
Type set in Rosemary Roman/Zurich BT

ISBN: 978-0-7643-3945-5

Printed in United States

Schiffer Books are available at special discounts for bulk purchases for sales promotions or premiums. Special editions, including personalized covers, corporate imprints, and excerpts can be created in large quantities for special needs. For more information contact the publisher:

Published by Schiffer Publishing Ltd.
4880 Lower Valley Road
Atglen, PA 19310
Phone: (610) 593-1777; Fax: (610) 593-2002
E-mail: Info@schifferbooks.com

For the largest selection of fine reference books on this and related subjects, please visit our website at **www.schifferbooks.com**
We are always looking for people to write books on new and related subjects. If you have an idea for a book, please contact us at
proposals@schifferbooks.com

This book may be purchased from the publisher.
Include $5.00 for shipping.
Please try your bookstore first.
You may write for a free catalog.

In Europe, Schiffer books are distributed by
Bushwood Books
6 Marksbury Ave.
Kew Gardens
Surrey TW9 4JF England
Phone: 44 (0) 20 8392 8585; Fax: 44 (0) 20 8392 9876
E-mail: info@bushwoodbooks.co.uk
Website: www.bushwoodbooks.co.uk

Acknowledgments

We would like to sincerely thank all of those who sent us e-mails over the past twelve years. This book would not have been possible without them.

It takes a lot of courage to first experience the unknown and then to share that experience with others. These e-mails will give the reader a unique view of the paranormal world through those who experienced them first hand.

We greatly appreciate all the support over the years and look forward to receiving many more e-mails!

Note from the Publisher:

This book includes sample submissions from over 11,000 emails to the authors over a twelve-year period. They are raw, without editing, spell-checking, changes, formatting, or grammatical corrections, and are presented in a what you see is what you get style to give the reader of a sense of the varied backgrounds involved with ghost investigative groups. Personal identities and locations have been changed to protect senders.

Contents

The official logo of the SWPRG.

Introduction

The Southern Wisconsin Paranormal Research Group (SWPRG) is a team of paranormal investigators and researchers who investigate paranormal activity as it relates to ghosts and hauntings.

The SWPRG team members are trained to use scientific methods and information to conduct serious paranormal investigations, which are comprised of conducting research, developing and testing theories, producing data and analysis-oriented results, providing resolution information, and encouraging public understanding and awareness. The team has investigated public and private locations all over the United States, from huge abandoned prisons and hospitals to private residences.

People worldwide contact the SWPRG for various reasons: to ask a question, make a comment, tell a story, request information, express interest in becoming a member, request a media interview and/or request an investigation be done in their home or business. "First contact" in most situations is via e-mail. These e-mails are then placed in the "e-file" for follow-up.

A good number of these e-mails can be "interesting" to say the least. Actually, they are so interesting that we thought others would find them fascinating to read...and there are plenty to pick from to share with you.

Looking over emails from the last 12 years, we found over 11,000 e-mails, and out of these, approximately 800 were suitable for publishing. And by suitable we mean: interesting, entertaining, creepy, scary, silly, and a special section that we call "'WTF?" – which really puts the "WHAT?" in WTF?

Not all 800 could be published in this book but the e-mails within were some of the best we have received! What makes them so good? These are the RAW e-mails! No editing! No changes! No formatting! No spell checking! No grammar corrections! That's right, what you see here is what we saw! What you see is what you get (with the exception of their personal identities and locations being changed).

These e-mails have been grouped into categories that we thought were suitable (even though a vast majority could just go in the "WTF?" section).

So, enjoy reviewing the e-mails that follow. We hope that you will find them as "interesting" as we did when we first got them.

With that being said, welcome to our world!

Chapter 1

Who Ya Gonna Call?

This chapter focuses on emails we received from people requesting a paranormal investigation of their property. They describe why they want an investigation and give details of what they have been experiencing that prompted them to contact us.

To Much To Handle!

Thursday, January 28, 2010 1:29 PM
From: Sarah, Madison, WI

I was wondering if there could be any sort of activity going on in the apartment that my boyfriend and I live in. We have had friends tell us they have heard cubboard doors slamming shut, I have been locked out of the apartment (we have a deadbolt and I was the only one here), the dishwasher has been unlocked and opened, and my computer has been turned on and logged in somehow without anybody putting the password in. My boyfriend has also said that there are nights that he is scared, actually scared. He has said that he needs to go to bed because he wants to die in his sleep, and that he doesnt want to see it. I also have scratches that appear on me out of nowhere.

Investigator Comments:

This is one of those cases that we would need more details on to be able to get a better understanding of the situation. Based on what was told to us, it appears it could be some sort of poltergeist activity, otherwise known as Recurrent Spontaneous Psychokinesis, which is a result of the living and has nothing to do with your typical "dead-guy" ghost.

Graves at local cemetery.

Ghosts in the House

Friday, August 21, 2009 12:46 PM
From: Tina, Madison, WI

Hi my name is Tina I'am 40 years old and I live in madison wi. On wednesday my daughter was in the shower when I heard her screaming. I thought it was probably a bug she was screaming about. I ran into the bathroom to see what the matter was and was totally unprepared for what she did say. She said there had been a lady standing in the bathroom. When I asked her what she looked like she described in very good detail what the lady looked like. When I asked her if the lady said anything to her or if she seemed like a nice lady she told me she was not. My daughter says the lady seemed to glare at her but that the lady had no eyes. I asked her if the "ghost" looked see through or like she was blurry and my daughter said no. My daughter isnt the type of child to make up stories and the fact that she was very scared and crying led me to believe that she had actually saw something or someone. In another instince I was in the shower late at night and I felt a prescence in the bathroom to the point that I felt I needed to get out of there. I have always felt like I had a **sixth sense** when it comes to spirits or ghosts and I feel something in this house. I would very much like to know if there is something here so that I can sleep at night and so that my children will be able to sleep as well.

Investigator Comments:

Cue Rockwell, "I always feel like somebody's watching me"...Sounds like you have a peeping paranormal pervert! Human beings can experience strange feelings when they are vulnerable...in this case, while in the shower. There may not necessarily be anything paranormal or abnormal about this particular situation but with the other things happening, it would be an interesting case to investigate.

Investigation Needed ... PRONTO!

Saturday, July 18, 2009 1:56 PM
From: Marsha, Door County, WI

Hi, My name is Marsha and I am an investor who lives in Door County. I am wondering if you would be able to help me get rid of a spirit that is in my home? I have had another Paranormal Society come over once already. They did hear many odd sounds and they also heard a girl singing while they were sitting in my living room, but their equipment for some reason did not pick up anything. I have been followed by some of the same spirits for the past 12 years, living in 4 different residences. I have tried many different things to get rid of them, such as moving away, saging, having my house blessed, and having psychics come in to help me tell them to leave.

I had 4 spirits here at one point. I have been told that 2 of them have successfully left, that the spirit of my daughter still visits only occassionally, and that one spirit remains. I have been told by several psychics that he is connected to my father in some way. One person told me that he may be a friend of my Dad's from an orphanage that he lived in until he was 7.

This man died young and he is very street smart—knowing when to not show himself. He was a prankster in life and he likes to bother only me. He likes to see my reactions. They told me that he thinks all of this is funny. He does not want to leave.

My husband works nights and I am often alone with my 2 young sons... This makes it very frightening for me. Here are some of the things that I have been experiencing:

*I smell very strong cigarette smoke some nights, even though no one in my house smokes.

*I have often felt someone bumping into my bed while I am sleeping and it wakes me up.

*I, on occassion, feel spirits poking me while I sleep.

*I have heard voices, like a man saying "AH!" in my face to wake me up while I am sleeping and I have also been woken up to my name being called.

*I sometimes hear loud cracks in the wall, and sounds as if someone is punching the wall very hard.

*On a few occassions while I was trying to fall asleep, I saw a very bright white flash of light. One night right after the flash of light, the window cracked so loudly two times that my son asked if someone had thrown a rock at it.

*Many, many of my shirts have at least one or two small holes in the bottom front of the shirt. Three psychics have told me that this is from the ghost's cigarettes......

*I "sense" the spirit standing in my bedroom door or next to my bed and I sometimes hear the floor creak (one part of the floor in the doorway to my room creaks when you step on it).

*I sometimes smell smoke in other areas of my house, but the activity has mostly only been in my bedroom while I sleep.

*One psychic that came over during the day, also said that my basement was "really bad".

In my last house I felt someone whack me on the elbow very hard while I was trying to fall asleep one night. I also felt the sheets being pulled off of me one night, and I heard far away childlike voices one evening on a few occassions (this was in the early evening while I was the only person in the house). I would also be woken up to someone tapping on either the back of my head or poking at my buttocks (3 pokes on one cheek and then 3 on the other). I also smelled the cigarette smoke there, as well.

Someone referred me to their psychic. She came over one night in March and she could feel the energy of spirits in different parts of my home and 2 of them showed themselves to her while we were sitting in our living room, one of them getting right up in her face (the one that is still here). She did try to tell him to leave, but we just heard a very loud thud in the wall and she said he was mad that we told him that.

A different psychic that has helped me get rid of the other 2 spirits that were here (one in Jan of 08 and one in April of 09), swears that there are no more spirits left in my home. I still smell smoke, I still sometimes get holes in my shirts, and I still sense him here. The psychic and her psychic friends also say that he remains. She told me that this spirit would be hard to get rid of and that she thought I would need a team of people to get him to go. She was in the process of getting this team together and now she has had a family crisis and has moved away. I really need help. Can you help me?

Thank you so much,

Investigator Comments:

After reading this initial email, some of our thoughts regarding this possible case were: First of all, the goal of the SWPRG is not to get rid of ghosts, but rather to seek out and try to understand strange phenomena. Second, this person mentioned moving away and we would never recommend that anyone leave their home due to possible paranormal activity. This is unrealistic...especially in this housing market! Third, in regards to their experiences when falling asleep or upon just wakening this could be due to hypnopompic and/or hypnagogic hallucinations which is simply a transitional state between wakefulness and sleep. Due to the expectations of what the client wanted and what we do, unfortunately, we were unable to accommodate this client.

Town Spook!

Wednesday, September 17, 2008 10:29 AM
From: Maggie, Delavan, WI

I have had a repoter from the newspaper come to my house to do a story about the ghost today and she told me that i should contact a paranormal investigater. i have ahd alot of "happenings" in my house from creepy feelings, hearing a male voice, my television turned on by itself, i have felt someone or something touch my feet as i was laying in bed (wide awake), my kids have seen and heard things. when i go down to my basement to do laundry i feel like someone is standing right behind me breathing on my neck, i turn to see if someone is there and there is no one there. there are slot of stuff happening here and i need your help, please. the reporter and myself would like to get to the bottom of this. i emailed my local historical society to find out the history on my house, but have not heard back from them yet. i get a feeling form these experiences that someone may have been killed here. PLEASE HELP ME.

Investigator Comments:

We took this case and drove to the clients home for a pre-investigation. When we got there, we were met by the media with a ton of questions as to what we thought was happening. They already had the expectation of the house being haunted and a story already half written. When the pre-investigation was concluded, we found there to be several natural explanations for the events. Due to our experiences with this case, we no longer take cases were the media has been called first.

Help!!

Wednesday, February 3, 2010 2:07 PM
From: Joseph

I had sent a email in care of the administrator per your research group email address, with more details. I had previously been in contact with a "Dave".

I'm writing now and left a voicemail per my son's request today. He said whatever is in his house has taken a toll for the worse and they need help now!! Whatever it is in the house is now going through the small children.

My grandson told his teacher they are coming to kill his dad, my approx. 18mo. old granddaughter last night told her mother in clear english she was going to die!! This baby can't speak clear words yet. This is also the child that whom or whatever is in the house threw her across the living room floor a few nights ago. She was not hurt just shaken up.

It also has made attemps to rape Tammy {my daughter – inlaw}. It has forcibly pinned down my son which is 9th degree black belt, and also has wittnessed its appearance, it has forcibly pinned down Tammy and little Jake{5yrs. old}. It is throwing things down and accross the rooms. Many other things. My son claims whatever this is is very strong!!!

It is believed to have come from Tammy's mother's home in Southern IL., where she visited at the beginning of the year. Her home has been confirmed haunted with a evil spirit named "Frank" which killed his wife & daughter and then committed suicide. Since Tammy's return to thier home in Janesville, there has been no reported activity at her mother's home.

Please refer to my original email and feel free to call me or my son at ANYTIME! We all live in the area in a Mobile Home Park. They have requested I contact you and set up for an investigation ASAP!!!

Investigator Comments:

We felt this case was serious and needed attention. Unfortunately, the people who were actually experiencing the phenomena were not interested in having us come out and do an investigation. The mother was not happy about it, but in the end, it was ultimately their decision.

Someone has to give us some sense to this. I can't sleep!

Monday, October 12, 2009 10:31 PM
From: Craig, South Beloit, WI

My name is Craig, My family and I live in South Beloit IL. We have lived here for about 2 1/2 years. We purchased this home from friends of ours. We have heard stories from them and their experiences with this house when they lived in it. During a certain time of the day (mid afternoon) they would hear a whistle and scratches on the wall during different times. This has happened to them for almost 7 years when they lived here. Anohter friend of mine spent the night here and was in the living room and seen a rocking chair rock back and forth for no reason. The owner of the house was in his daughter's room reading to her just before bedtime, and they had a dresser in the room. Each handle flicked up one by one and he said he sat there and didn;t know what to think. Another night, they had friends come over for a card game. One of their friends is a psychic and she came along for the card game. No one had told her about this house and the events that have gone on. Once she walked into the house, she told them something was there, that it wasn't bad and that it seemed good. There also was a little boy that was with the group. The front porch door was open, and this little boy looked over from the chair he was sitting in and seen this old man with a hat on and looking at him, just sitting there on one of the wicker couches on the porch. This little kid freeked out and climbed over his mother to get away from this older man. So I asked what happened afte that. They told me that this kid said that he seen this man sitting there and all the sudden this man was right in front of him... face to face. This is why we freeked out so bad.

They began to tell their psychic friend what has been going on in the house for a long time, they just didn't say anyhing to anyone because maybe no one believe them. They even had 3 cats in the house and most of the time they lived in the basement. No cat has ever come flying up from the basement or even acted strange in the house. We all think that if pets don't see anything, than there shouldn't be anything around.

Ever since that psychic came through the house, just her presence or something, nothing has happened in the house for a year. Well, me and my wife decided to buy it from our friends.

About a year went by, and it all started.......I guess I never paid attention to it. At the same time, I never felt easy about going to the basement. This house is 108 years old. Very nice house. The basement is old and damp. It even has a "tomb room" as we call it. This is the room that is towards the back of the basement and it was used back in the old days where they brought the Cole in from outside.

Sometimes I would go to bed and I can't fall asleep because once I start to doze off, I would feel a thump on the bed as if someone walked into the bed and bumped it. I would yell at my wife because she is a constant mover. It would happen from time to time for the last 1 1/2 years or so. I too, would hear that whistle during the daytime. It was like it was right in the house. Weird right?

My 13 year old daughter was down in the basement just last week doing laundry, and she seen out of other corner of her eye, someone jumped off the last couple steps onto the basement floor. She said who ever it was had blue jeans on and maybe a black shirt. She said she didn't't know if it was a man or woman. It happened so fast and it was gone. She said she seen it, but didn't freak out and she finished loaded the washer and came up stairs and told me right away about it. That night, I went to bed and I was listening to my talk show radio on my head phones. I went to bed around 2:30am like I usually do. I do photography work, so the only time I have is later at night after all these kids go to bed. Anyway... I'm laying there for not even 10 minutes and I feel that "THUMP" on the bed. I am laying on my side facing my wife and I'm like "what the hell". I open my eyes and I seen my wife walking from the bed towards the door. But the door didn't open. I kinda shut my eyes and opened them again because I figured that she would have opened the door. I kinda sat up to look over towards the door and I didn;t see her, but I did... she was still laying next to me in bed... in the same position as she was when I got in the room. Covers were still next to her face exactly as they were. I could see she didn't move at all. When I laid there and seen this... I know someone was in the room. I seen it so vividly, that's why I thought it was her. Little light coming in from the window because of the street light. We also have the hallway light on and the door was pushed shut, but not latched. This allowed the light to come through the door crack. This image was in the room because the light from the hallway was blocked by someone as it walked in the way of that door. I laid there and I shut my eyes. I knew what I seen. I rolled over. I wasn't freaked out. It was weird. I was able to go to sleep like in 15 minutes.

I told my wife about it the next day. She knew about what happened to my daughter when she was doing laundry. See... my wife hears everyone's else's stories...but never believes it. She laughs at it....Until now.......

She said " I wasn't going to say anything until now. I was in the basement last night and I heard something fall in the tomb room, and it was loud. I knew it wasn't something up stairs." I said to her "Are you believing this stuff now?".

All I know, I can't sleep in the house. I have a hard time. I leave all the lights on, keep my door open and have one of my dogs sleep in the hallway. I know lights may not matter, but it helps me. It's like I'm a kid and scared of the dark. Stuff has gone on in the house for a long time. Than time went on and nothing. Now, it starts again...little things, thumping on the bed for over a year when I thought it was my wife the whole time. Now, we are starting to see someone. I have no idea if it is a man or woman. It's like it's getting worse, now we can see them? That night in my room.. I couldn't tell if it was a man or woman. I just assumed it was my wife.. who else could it be right? She even told me that she felt the same thump on the bed for 3 nights in a row about a week ago.

So far, it seems that no one knows the history on this house. I haven't went to the city office to get info...past owners or anything.

Please come and do your thing. I want to see if you find anything, see anything.... this house is yours. Do what you have to do, do what you want. We are going to move or something. I can't live in this house with this stuff going on.

So when can you come? Yesterday? Please respond ASAP!!!!!

Investigator Comments:

The owners came in with preconceived notions of this house already being haunted. It doesn't mean that what they experienced wasn't real, but when natural phenomena happens, it can be misinterpreted as paranormal and can raise the stress levels of the people involved. This, coupled with the waking/sleeping hallucinations we discussed in an earlier case, can certainly make for a frightening situation. Not to say that everything going on here can be explained naturally, but we need to rule natural phenomena out before considering a paranormal explanation.

My Son

Wednesday, August 27, 2008 8:13 PM
From: Sharon, Beloit, WI

Hello sorry to bother you but i dont know what else to do,my family and i just moved into this house on the east side of beloit,and my son will be playing in the backyard or even in the house and hes laughing and talking with someone,I know what your thinking all kids have imaganary friends but this is different he will be nine in november and he has cognitive disabilites basically he has hard time reading,writing,and speech,but there are some things hes saying when i listen in that he just doesnt hear everyday if at all,for instince i asked him who hes talking to he told me guy said he was standing right next to me in broad day light okay then he walks to the yard and said his brains are here he has black hole in his head someone shot him through the eye he said to me,okay we dont hunt the most violent thing he watches is spongebob and wrestling he listens to country music and some rock,but where he got that from i dont know then yesterday he was playing on swing set and i seen him looked like someone picked him up and threw him he got up and was crying and swinging his fist telling something to go home,he came in and he had red marks on his arms and one scratch on his nose,please tell me im not crazy,I belive in alot and have lived in haunted homes before but never had a home feel like this and physical harm to some one what can i do please help me Im scared to try things on my own dont want to anger anything,there is some thing in basement here,you always get the feeling your being watched,but my son has never been like this before if you can help i would forever be greatful to you,thank you Sharon

Investigator Comments:

We took this case and did a complete investigation. The following conclusion was that due to the fact there is considerable stress for the family due to the recent move, the murder of an acquaintance, the death of a dog, the eight year old boy having cognitive disabilities, the clients lack of sleep and having to take medication for it could certainly be playing a role in the perceiving and interpretation of the reported paranormal experiences. A paranormal causation for the reported activity is not supported at this time. The confounding factors mentioned above and the potential role of the electromagnetic fields and high positive ion counts in the basement further enhanced and confused the situation. This is not to say that the experiences she and her family have had are not real (especially the boy reportedly being thrown). However, in order to further determine the cause of the reported subjective paranormal experiences it is first necessary for the client to work with her physician(s) to resolve her seizure, stress and sleep issues. The client is urged to continue to keep a journal of the experiences they have and stay in touch with the SWPRG.

Cleanse This House!

Thursday, January 31, 2008 2:57 AM
From: Janine, East Troy, WI

I live in a haunted house that is getting more and more activity the longer we live here.We were just experiencing seeing shadows and people walking aroung out of the corner of our eyes,cold spots,night mares,and feeling someone standing right beside us.Recently,the entity has been holding down my daughter and fiance at wee hours in the morning. Like suffocating ,holding down in bed where they're not able to say anything or call out for help.Please contact me via email or by phone. I would like you to come investigate and cleanse this home.

Thanks.

Investigator Comments:

We don't do cleansings, windows, or laundry. *Nuff* said!

Gift or Curse?

Tuesday, January 29, 2008 5:05 PM
From: Bob, Evansville, WI

I just got a call from Yuri who found us on the internet. His wife is having issues with "seeing spirits". He says that she see's them everywhere and needs help figuring out what to do with this "gift/curse".

Do yo have anyone that might be able to investigate this and perhaps help them out? Yuri called me and seems pretty concerned. He also told me story about a house he lived in, in Belvidere, Illinois. He says they needed help with a spirit in the house and they found a person named "Annette" or however you spell it. In any event, the lasdy came out and charged them $500 to "cross him over". I told him that no legitimate paranormal investigation team would charge for somethime like that. So be cautious, they have already been burned once.

I have some other teams helping track the $500 ghostbuster down so we can see who this is and expose her. But if you can help Yuri and his wife out they would really appreciate it.

Thanks for your time. Please let me know if you decide to help or not so I can keep trying till I find another reputable team in th area to help.

Thanks!

Investigator Comments:

$500 bucks?? Holy ecto slimer! Unfortunately, we tried several times to contact this potential client, but never received an email back. Sometimes that's just the way these emails go.

Can't Sleep.....

Wednesday, January 23, 2008 10:10 PM
From: Bobby Jo, Milwaukee, WI

I woke up one night itching my arm, and when I woke I felt bumps the size of small beeds on my right arm, this isn't the first time this has happened to me. Other nights I wake up crying or scared. I have even felt really cold, I told myself that it was only me and to go back asleep, but then a few night before I had woke up with the bumps on my arm, I was being choked by something, I woke up and couldn't breath. I thought maybe it was me and it was just a bad dream!, but every time I goto bed I ask my boyfriend to leave the bedroom door open cuz I don't feel safe in the room with it shut!, Last night was the worst cuz I felt that someone was watching me, so I shouted for my boyfriend and he couldn't hear me and I started to cry cuz I felt like was being held down, so I couldn't get up and get out of our room! When I shouted for him for the 3rd time he hurd me, asked me what was wrong but all I could do was cry, then I told him that I was being held down and felt like I couldn't get up! He stayed in the room with me till I fell back asleep. This hasn't happened to me before, it was always cold in my room and I learned to ignore it. But it all got worse when I found out I was Pregnet, I am 1 1/2 month along now. Im very worried for myself my boyfriend and the new baby on the way!! If you would please eather e-mail me back or call me ASAP would be best!!

Thank You Very Much

Investigator Comments:

This sounds like a very natural phenomena called, "Old Hag Syndrome." This is experienced when your body is in a state of paralysis that is normally associated with sleep at the same time you are beginning to wake up. It can last a few seconds to several minutes, but soon passes. You feel like your awake, but your body hasn't caught up just yet. It can be accompanied by visual and auditory hallucinations and can be extremely frightening and feel very real. This is a very natural phenomena and tends to happen to many people. It would be best to consult with the family physician in a case like this especially since they are pregnant and reported a skin condition.

Cell Phone Message

Monday, November 19, 2007 7:20 PM
From: Samantha, Wausau, WI

My 21 year old son passed away unexpectedly in my home aug 1, two days after his 21st birthday from a childhood heart complication. I have had many obvious signs of him, but the most recent other than my usual light bulb problem, is a cell phone message from him you can clearly hear some of what he is saying, (a lot of "mom" s) but much of it is very high pitched screatching. I was wondering if you had any type of equipment that would help me understand more of the message. Im sure he's telling me he's ok and he clearly says i love you in the message. Im not into its the devil kind of thing or demonic possesions, i accually love to get his signs and dont need it to go away or anything, I just need some help with the message. I believe deeply in ghosts are ones who dont know they are dead, or who refuse to cross over, and spirits are around us contacting us from the other side, i believe he is a spirit contacting me happily, making sure all his family and friends are dealing with this and he's ok. He knew i was very open to the spirit world and he knows i would except his signs. However, obviously i am very anxious to find out ALL that was said on my message, to make sure everything really is ok. Ive lived in my apartment for two years and have never had any bad vibes so to speak, theres been nothing but a plesant feeling here, and there still is, so no devil here, no weegee board demons,curses or possesions, sorry if your disappointed, but i can give you some very interesting signs he's given me, his sister and some of his friends that were afraid and hesitant to mention to me.

Investigator Comments:

It's so sad when you lose a child. We did analyze this message and it does sound like someone saying, "I Love You!" It seems as if the bond between a mother and her son can't be broken even in death.

Dead Phone!

Thursday, April 19, 2007 12:09 PM
From: Matt, LaCrosse, WI

I am having alot of strange occurances that are really getting out of hand. What stareted out as doors opening and closing have now graduated to footsteps upstairs,smells,and balls bouncing in the basement. I also have some disturbing pics and video of something I filmed with the cam-corder.I was recording one of my dogs and several times you can see something move across the screen. But it isn't just that, there is definately something here and I have a feeling it doesn't know it's gone. I hear footsteps at pretty much the same time during the day and evening. I smell perfumes and somke and I have literally watched the livingroom fan-light cord being pulled down on a daily basis. Every time I have tried to dial the telephone number on you website, the phone would ALWAYS be dead. ALWAYS. I need some help here because it is only getting worse. If you think you can help please call or e-mail me ASAP

Investigator Comments:

We did finally get in touch with this person via telephone. I remember being on the phone with this person and the phone did hang up twice, which was not at the hand of either the client or myself. We recommended this person keep a journal of what is happening and when. She did. She called me several weeks later and said, "I don't know what you did, but it has all stopped." We hear this remark a lot. We don't usually do anything specific with the case, rather it is due to the stress level of the person involved usually feeling better about the fact they have been in contact with us and the situation will sometimes either resolve itself or come back after a length of time. We never heard from this person again. So, we can only assume it resolved itself.

Rumor Has It, The Place Is Haunted!

Saturday, May 20, 2006 6:50 AM
From: Angie, Augusta, WI

We bought this house in Nov.2005 and have had numerous experiences here since we moved in. This is I am told the oldest or second oldest house in town being built in 1893.A few occurances such as daughters being tucked in tight with blankets to their neck,being zipped up in a sleeping bag overnight when they were not "inside it" when they went to sleep,furnace being turned up all the way for no reason,heavy candle flying off and hitting me in leg,water bowl flying off table and across room on its own in front of us,the sound of children laughing and playing when I was alone in house,daughters have seen a black figure numerous times,tv going off then on again and channels changing on their own.Temperature differance upstairs colder than rest of the house also.We do have pics with lots of orbs and one with a real strange bright splash of light in it when no light was on there.

Please contact me for we would like to know if something is really here.Rumors in town is that this place is haunted. Thanks

Investigator Comments:

With experiences like that, it's no wonder the place is thought to be haunted!

Open THAT...You're DEAD!

Wednesday, October 26, 2005 12:38 AM
From: Oscar, Janesville, WI

Hello,

I just bought a house built around 1890 and have experienced some very unusual stuff. After a door opened that I knew I shut. I slammed it shut and yelled out "open that bitch!, you're dead". About an hour later I was laying down in a dreamy state and a ghostly figure came straight for me. Another time I was arriving home after walking my dog and I saw something move from the bottom of the first floor window go up towards the ceilling. I met my neighbors and they asked me if I've experienced anything abnormal. They told me that the previous owners thought there was a old woman and a tempermental old man in the house. I don't think this is my mind playing a trick on me and I'd really like to have it investigated.

Thanks.

Investigator Comments:

One question...Did the door ever open again after that? That's all I wanna know!

Smells Like Grandma

Wednesday, August 31, 2005 7:09 PM
From: Sharon, Waukesha, WI

My mother and i have been having Paranormal activity in our house for about 8 months and we told them to go away and basically they did, but they let us know that they are still here and still aware that we are here. They have not tried to harm us in anyway, but in the main room at least 2 times a month we can smell some purfume like my grandmother used to wear. My mother and I would like you to investigate this activity. It hasnt been happening as much as it did but every onve in a while they come back. The "spirit" is usually here on Friday and Saturday nights. Please contact us about this situation. Thank you.

Investigator Comments:

Friday and Saturday nights are good with us! Bring it on! Scents are frequently reported in haunted locations, even more so than seeing an apparition. If it is happening on a certain day and time, perhaps it is a residual haunting, which is simply a moment captured in time and is played back under the right conditions. Things slowed down so we didn't investigate. Maybe when the activity picks up again we will do an investigation.

Super Sensitive Wiccan

Sunday, August 28, 2005 6:07 AM
From: Jody, Milwaukee, WI

Hi, I am Wiccan and am also sensitive to spirits.The past two and a half years or so I have been taking pictures at night in local cemetaries. And so far I have been very lucky with the pictures that I get. I have alot of pictures of orbs and I have been lucky enough to get some full manefestations. I thought that I would try something different about 4 or 5 months ago when the apartment downstairs from me was empty again. You see, the lower flat below mine has alot of people moving in and out of it (in fact they should put a revolving door on that place as often as it empties out.) But anyway, usually when empty my son and I have been designated to watch over the apartment for the owners and have quite often heard some pretty weird stuff coming from the place at night.So when these last people moved out we started going in at night, I would set up my candles and I tried a spirit summoning spell in there to try to see what exactly it was we hear all the time. Well, the most we heard was heavy breathing and footsteps in the basement and in the kitchen and on a couple of occasions we heard the basement door try to be opened. You see there are locks on the basement door because almost everyone that has lived down there have been afraid of the basement.I decided to leave a tape recorder running in there all night just to see what I could catch. Well, I have 1 tape that has something saying something but I can't quite make it out and also things moving around in the apartment and what sounds to be like doors being closed. Which my son and I knew this was impossible because we were the only ones with a key except the landlords and they live pretty far from us. and everytime anyone moves out he changes the locks the same day. This is where you come in. I want to find out if you people do stuff with sound if so can you help me please.

Thank you. By the way I have one enlarged picture you folks might be interested in seeing. Please contact me. best time is early in the morning or between 5 and 9:30 at night.

Investigator Comments:

This email gives us the opportunity to comment on orbs. 99.9% of orbs can be explained naturally. Pictures taken outside at night are most likely bugs or pollen. It's very important to be able to control your conditions whenever possible and rule out all natural explanations first.

Spook Eyed

Thursday, February 5, 2004 8:39 AM
From: Sarah, Superior, WI

We purchased this 100 year old farm in Dodge county out of watertown and my daughter is living there. there are many strange things happening, including opening the door on the fire furnace in the basement that has a fool latch that can not open by itself. There was a shadow in front of the lightbulb lastnight in the basement that moved away. It was as if someone was standing in front of the lightbulb and then stepped away so you could see the lightbulb. When she is in the basement, there is furniture moving across the floor in the Kitchen overhead. And she is alone in the house. When she is in the main floor things are crashing in the basement, when she goes down, nothing is moved. Last night her cat jumped off the bed, and began following movement like she was watching a fly buzz around and then the cat came flying back in the bedroom afraid and all spook eyed.

Sandy is getting very nervous is there some way you can check this out. This only happens when she is alone, when the kids or Doug are home, nothing happens at all. you have to contact me email as she is not on line.

Thank you

Investigator Comments:

Sounds like an excellent case. Unfortunately, we were unable to talk with Sandy.

Are We Crazy?

Friday, November 28, 2003 8:36 AM
From: Suzanne, Monroe, WI

we have been at this house for 3 years. i would like to know for sure if what we are seeing and feeling are the previous owners, or if we are just plain crazy. we have a lot of information, pictures, names, and documented stories and events of the family that lived here before us. we need profesional help!!

Investigator Comments:

People contact us frequently because they want to know they aren't crazy. Many people have experiences they can't explain. That's what keeps us in business. Sometimes, just talking with someone about what is happening and knowing others have similar experiences is all it takes to make one feel better.

Old Hag Syndrome

Monday, October 14, 2002 12:12 AM
From: Mitsy, Dodgeville, WI

I am just curious about your investigations. How long do you spend on one? Do you always bring in a psychic? I know that our house is haunted, we don't actually need anymore proof. I would truly like to know how many spirits there are and why they are staying here.

We moved into our home 12 years ago and have had many periods of almost constant activity. We have also had long periods of none at all. I would like to find out why they come and go like they do. There have been times that we have all slept in the living room because we didn't want to be separated. Right now the activity level is fairly low. nothing more than bumping sounds and things moving once in a while Three years ago at this time we actually considered leaving it was so bad.

I am worried that it will happen again. My 15 year old daughter hasn't slept more than a handful of nights in her own room since she was 3. She seems to be the "target" when things get out of hand. She also has sleep paralysis episodes and semi-wake visual experiences. Recently she was in such a state when she saw a young girl lean over her and heard her whisper in her ear, "check your left ear" The girl then disapeared. When my daughter checked, all the earrings from her left ear were gone. She had been wearing three in each ear, we never found them. She has had sudden scratches appear on her arms, had her room completely trashed, including furniture overturned when no one was in the room. We all have had our problems here but she seems to take the brunt of it. I wouldn't mind having an investigation done here but we would also like some answers if possible. I would be happy to try and make a list of the things we have witnessed and heard if you would be interested. We also have several pictures of orbs, faces, mists...etc. The clearest one we have is of a cat sitting in the attic, its as if it is staring right at the camera but you can see through it. Would you be interested? Thanks

Investigator Comments:

Our investigation process consists of a few different steps. First we will do a pre-investigation which is when two investigators will come to your home, ask you to describe what you have been experiencing and show us where things are happening. We will then take environmental readings to rule out any natural phenomena and try to fully understand what it is you have been experiencing. This usually takes about 2 hours or so. If we feel we need to do more investigating, we will follow it up with a full investigation which is a more comprehensive version of the pre-investigation. We follow that up with the reveal which is simply sitting down with the client to explain what we found. We don't usually use psychics in our investigations, therefore we would not be able to tell them how many spirits are in their home or why they are there.

Lots to Deal With

Sunday, July 28, 2002 1:43 PM
From: Keith and Amanda, Oshkosh, WI

Moderate poltergeist-type activity, objects moved, things dropped from shelves. Animals in the house (one dog and one cat) will sometimes get very edgy for no apparent reason, and sometimes stare and growl at one wall in particular, even though no one was in the room. One of the objects moved was a relatively heavy cast-iron coin bank. Our son, Adam, is 18 months old and is sometimes awakened at night in what seems to be a night terror, and also usually points at the same wall, or area that the pets seem to be suspicious of. We have also experienced odd noises at night, a rhythmic tapping, usually two to four times in a row, that seem to move throughout the house. These types of "abnormal" activities have been increasing in frequency and now sometimes occur during the day. We would appreciate hearing from your organization regarding our phenomenon.

Investigator Comments:

We thought this was a very interesting case and were interested in taking it. We were in contact on several occasions with the individuals in this case, however, an investigation was never performed at this location. Unfortunately, this happens in many cases.

Chapter Two

If We Had a Nickle For Every Time We Were Asked...

This chapter focuses on emails we received from people who have questions about a variety of different paranormal related topics.

It's Just Like the Show, "A Haunting"

Sunday, July 15, 2007 8:56 PM
From: Beth, Oregon, WI

I have been recently hooked on the t.v. show on the Discovery Channel called A Haunting. After watching it was hooked on it and have seen different types of hauntings etc., as of recently my boyfriend and I have been experencing various abnormal activity. I tried doing some research about it and believe that It may possibly be a form of a poltergeist. I have been experiencing things such as the door slamming shut out of nowhere, while driving in my boyfriends car the doors will unlock and all of his windows will roll down as well as the sun roof opening up, and also we both have a weird feeling of being watched. Do you think that you may be able to help me better understand what is going on and if i may be going crazy Thanks

Investigator Comments:

It is interesting that the activity started after she began watching the paranormal TV shows. We've heard many times of people watching a scary movie or paranormal TV show and then having a supernatural experience. A few different things could be going on here:

1. By watching the shows, people become primed and look for a weird experience and subsequently misperceive and/or misinterpret some natural phenomena;

2. They become scared and stressed, and the result is poltergeist activity; or

3. They know what to look for and do experience genuine paranormal activity.

Regardless of what the answer is, one must remain critical of the TV shows and what they experience.

Da da da da da da da da da…Ratman!

Tuesday, December 1, 2009 6:27 PM
From: Daniel, Libertyville, IL

I was wondering if you have ever heard of this or have any details on this....

I grew up in northeast Illinois in the Libertyville Illinois area which is just south of the Wisconsin/Illinois border and was really close to Great America (and I heard about some of great American being haunted as well so if you have any information on that I would appreciate it as well).

Amyway....my friends used to tell me that there was this creature/ghost/spirit called Ratman. Ratman was supposed to be a combination of a human with a rats head and had red eyes that you could see at night when he (or maybe a she) was staring at you while trying to probably hunt you. The Ratman was supposedly living in a park called Adler Park, which had lots of woods a swmming pool and kids used to have summer camp out there. They would even stay overnight and camp and they would report all kinds of weird stuff going on...most of it they thought was due to the Ratman, however they said maybe some of it was due to a ghost of a kid that was killed in the park. But most of what they said was that they saw this Ratman.

They said mostly at night that they would see the creepy red eyes of Ratman looking at them from off in the distance in the woods. They said those eyes would follow them pretty much as they moved from one place to another. If they tried to approach the eyes (for those who were brave or stupid enough to do that) the eyes would just disappear and they would hear something running off into the woods.

There was even this one friend of mine that said he saw Ratman in full daylight. He said the creature had a rats face... real long nose with whiskers coming out on both sides, pointed ears and beady little black rat eyes. His body looked like that of a human but he was kinda hunched over and had a hump in his back but he mostly walked upright. He seemed to run on two legs but would go down on all fours when he stopped. It was like he stopped and sniffed around to see who was there and what they was doing. He almost seemed liked he was checking peopke out and then kinda ran off they they saw what he was doin or thinking.

This really seemed to reak people out and a lot of the kids in the neighborhood were afraid to go to that park and really didn't wanna go there and stay overnight.

The Des Plains river ran thru the Adler Park area and went down by where my parents house was at the time. Well, one night I was on the phone with my friends and they were telling some Ratman stories when I looked out the window towards the river and the woods across the streeat and I couldn't believe it but I swear I saw these two little red eyes staring at me!!! I was inside the house but man I thought that thing was looking right at me. It was kinda like it knew we were talking about him. It scared the crap out of me. I was totally freaking out and was telling my friends about what I was seeing. They told me to get off the phone and run over there and see if I could find this creature Ratman. So, I got iff the phone and ran over to the river where I thought I saw this thing. There was nothing there when I got over there. So, I went home and called my friends back and told them I didn't find anything. The next day they came over and we went on a quest to try to find something that would prove that what I saw was really there. When we got back to that spot we looked around and saw some broken branches that could have been broken by the Ratman. We also saw some weird footprints that didn't look human but didn't look like an animal either. So we thought that was pretty cool.

When we were there looking for Ratman we also found what looked like a REALLY old tomb stone. I winder if it had anything to do with why the Ratman was there? Not sure but it could have. Maybe it was his grave or maybe it was someone he got to.

So, have you heard about the Ratman? What do you think it could be? Do you think it was a living creature? Or maybe it was a ghost of a creature? I wonder if it was related to a werewolf or maybe that beast of bray road thing that I have heard about in the Wisconsin area. Do you think it could possibly have been a demon or demonic? If so, I hope that I never encounter it again.

Just wondering if you have ever heard of this thing or have any idea what it may have been.

Thanks for your time and please let mw know what you thing.

Investigator Comments:

Ahhhhh....OK! Gonna forward this one to the Cryptozoologists. Thanks for your submission!

WildCat Mountain

Tuesday, May 15, 2007 3:19 PM
From: Stephanie, Madison, WI

I recently read an article dated October 26, 2006 regarding the haunting of Wild Cat Mountain. If you already have information or find something interesting regarding the ghost of WildCat Mountain please contact me. I'm intruiged.

Thank You

Investigator Comments:

Ummm...We got nothin'!

Ouija Board Shock

Sunday, December 11, 2010 5:23 AM
From: Jake, Janesville, WI

Just wondering what you thought about this thing that happened to me when I was a child. When I was 10 years old my family had a Ouija board in the house. I used to play with it and really didn't think much about it. It would sometimes seem to move on its own but who knows if someone else in the group playing with it moved it by themselves. So, I was never really convinced that there was much to this thing. But then something very strange happened...

One day I was playing with my BB/Pellet gun out in the back yard and needed something to shoot at as a target. I looked all over the house and finally came across the Ouija board. So, I thought this would make a good target. Besides, the thing never really worked anyway.

I took the board outside and put it on the fence. I then proceeded to shoot it up pretty good with the BB/Pellet gun. About 30 minutes later the Ouija board looked like a piece of swiss cheese. After inspecting my excellent marksmanship ability, I broke the board in half and threw it in the garbage. I then went inside.

I went to bed and the next day something very weird happened. I got up, had breakfast and then went downstairs to watch some television. I came down the stairs and saw something that was rather shocking! The OUIJA BOARD WAS ON THE COFFEE TABLE!!!!!! AND IT LOOKED LIKE NEW!!!!

This totally freaked me out because I knew we only had one Ouija board in the house and I am pretty sure that my parents didn't even know that I had taken it outside and shot it up!

Have you ever heard of anything like that before? Do you think there is something to those Ouija boards?

Thanks for your time!

Investigator Comments:

I think someone in the house is playing a trick on you. There is a stigma associated with Ouija boards that they can communicate with the dead. There is also the popular notion that devils or demons communicate through them and use them as a gateway to our world. We have never personally had any experiences, good or bad, with a Ouija board. These things are mainly for entertainment and there are many natural explanations for things that have said to have happened with them. This includes everything from ideomotor activity to fraud to trickery. But just to be safe, I wouldn't recommend busting a cap in the devils ass again! I assume that wouldn't help but only annoy him. I've heard he's a bit of a hot head.

Coffee Woods

Friday, May 11, 2007 6:57 PM
From: Jason, Evansville, WI

Have you ever looked into the haunted farmhouse in platteville? Whats this about the haunted subway in dodgeville? Also the woods outside of platteville may be haunted. The woods are known as "coffee woods."

Investigator Comments:

A few questions:

1. Which farmhouse would that be? There has to be more than one.

2. Which woods would that be? We know that there is a lot of farmland in Southern Wisconsin, but we're sure there is more than one wood lot. As far as the subway, we have heard it is haunted and we have eaten there, but did not have any experiences and have not done an investigation thus far.

Creepy Old House You Need to See!

Thursday, August 17, 2006 9:56 PM
From: Renee, Madison, WI

While I have no funds to pay for an investigation, there is a town called Rock Island, in Illinois in which resides an abandoned house that I camped out at with 2 other people while traveling. Although I am not sure what the exact address is, it is a gray house on a street with a deck that is falling apart.

To summarize, we had a very frightening night there, and we are most certain it is haunted. if you think to go, just ask the locals, when we told them we were just camping out in an abandoned house, they instantly advised against "the gray house", claiming that the place even creeps out the neighbors.

Investigator Comments:

Trespassing while "Camping" in an abandoned house, otherwise known as "squating," is illegal and not advisable. While no specifics are given on what happened that night, there is no doubt that it left a lasting impression. Perhaps the house was abandoned, but only by the living. Unfortunately, without having the address or permission of the owners, there is nothing we can do at this time.

Real paranormal equipment used by the SWPRG during investigations.

Paranormal Shows Versus Real Investigators

Wednesday, July 28, 2010 10:57 PM
From: Daniel, Jefferson, WI

Have you guys ever met Jason and Grant from TAPS? Or anyone else from TAPS? Have you ever worked with them on an investigation?

Have you ever met Ryan Buel from Paranormal State? Or Lorraine Warren? How about Chip "Hazelnut" Coffee from Psychic Kids? What do you think about these people or the shows they are on?? I watch those shows all the time and all I have to say is, "That's ALL FAKE". I think what you guys do is more realistic.

If I would ever meet any of those people, I would slap them right across their smug, arrogant, and stupid mouths! You guys' should be more upset about this crap than I am, but I'm FED UP with all the hype about how society respects the "TV SHOW STARS" more than the REAL researchers in this field!

Sorry to rant, but I just wanted you to know that I really respect what you guys do and feel bad that so many people take what they see on TV and think its how it really works.

Keep up the FANTASTIC WORK! We are all behind you!

Investigator Comments:

Answers: No. No. Yes. No. No. No. No. Entertainment. Remember, TV is for entertainment and there is much more to paranormal investigating. We appreciate all your support. It's good that they have brought more exposure to the field, but people must realize there is important, meaningful work being done by serious researchers. Thank you for your kind words and continued support.

Authentic Ouija Board.

Ouija Think About That?

Sunday, March 1, 2009 12:57 PM
From: Damien, Fond du lac, WI

Do you think Ouija Boards are for real?

I wanted to get you thoughts on that questions because I had some weird experiences with a Ouija board when I was in college.

I lived in a coed dorm during my sophomore year in college and I had a group of people that I would hang around with. One night we found out that one of the guys on the floor, Keith, has a Ouija board. He asked us if we wanted to play around with it. He said it was pretty cool and he was totally convinced that it worked. He said that when he was a young kid got in touch with a specific spirit that would answer all his questions. If he wanted to talk to his family members who had died this spirit would also go and 'get' them. He also said that he somewhat stopped using it cause strange things started happening in house. He said that objects in his bedroom would move around on their own, lights would go on and off by themselves, the TV would turn on and off, his closet door would open, he started hearing voices and he even said he felt like someone was there staring at him.

I didn't really think much of the Ouija Board and I didn't believe it worked and all those things he said happened were probably just stories, so why not go ahead and play around with thing.

We got 6 people from the dorm floor to try this thing out. We lit a few candles, sat around in a circle and Keith brought out the Ouija Board. I have to tell you that I almost laughed cause it was nothing more than the toy one that you can buy at some toy store. I was kinda expecting some ancient board from long ago that was owned by one of those witches in Salem. Anyway, he put the thing in the middle of the circle and two people put their fingers on the pointer – Keith and some girl.

About a minute later the pointer began to move and both swore that they weren't moving the pointer. Some people in the room started to get a little freaked out. The pointer was just sliding over the board and wasn't really spelling out or telling us anything. Then, some people started asking questions. After awhile we started getting yes and no answers. It seemed like they had made contact with the ghost of a little girl who lived in the area in the early 1900s and died of some sickness.

So, they started asking the little girl spirit more questions asking her to spell out answers using the letters on the board. However, they just kept getting yes and no answers.

Two different people wanted to see if it would work for them. Keith and this girl switched with two other people. And after a few minutes the pointer started to move again and giving yes and no answers. The two new people swore they were NOT moving the pointer.

After an hour of doing this they found out that the little ghost gril used to walk to school and lived in a small house not to far from her school. She said that a lot of people died this one year and a lot of her friends had died. She was very sad and was looking for her mom and dad. All of this was determined by asking the yes and no questions.

Now, something really weird happened…As they were playing with the Ouija board, one of the candles started to flicker like there was a strong breeze in the room. There should not have been a breeze since the dorm room door was closed and so was the window and this was the first time the candle did this after an hour. Finally the candle blew out!!! Of course the girls in the room screamed and said we should stop. They wanted to leave. Keith convinced them to stay a little bit longer and try it some more.

As they again changed the people at the board, the pointer seemed to move a little bit on its own. I didn't really see it but the others did and it did look like it was in a different position. At this point people thought enough was enough cause they were now getting a little freaked out. So, we put everything away, blew out the candles and everyone went back to their own rooms.

The next morning at breakfast Keith said he had some REALLY weird dreams about a little girl. He also said that he woke up and his folding closet door was open. He said he knew it was closed before he went to bed and there was no way he had opened it during the night. He was pretty freaked out because it seemed a lot like what had happened to him when he used to play with it as a little kid. We all asked him what he was going to do. He said he was going to go to church and get a little holy water and sprinkle it around his room…just to be safe. So, he did that and he said a little prayer and nothing else seemed to happen.

Everyone, except Keith, eventually wanted to play with the Ouija board again. Keith did NOT want to have anything to do with it. People played with it on and off for a few weeks but nothing ever happened- the pointer on the board never moved and nothing happened in any of their rooms.

It was weird but I am not sure if it was real or not.

Do you think Ouija Boards are real? Have you had any experience with it? Do you think people were just freaking themselves out? Could they have been moving it without knowing they were doing it? Just wondering what you think

Investigator Comments:

As we stated in a previous comment about Ouija boards, We have never personally had any experiences, good or bad. These things are mainly for entertainment and there are many natural explanations for things that have said to have happened with them. This includes everything from ideomotor activity to fraud to trickery. This could also be another case where having strong beliefs and expectations leads one to misinterpret or misperceive natural events. Whatever the case may be, we would love to be invited to the next Ouija board coed party. Giggity!

Chapter Three

Did I Eva Tell Ya'll Bout Da Time...

This chapter focuses on emails we received from people who have had real paranormal experiences. They have described every detail of their experience in order for us to understand their frustration, confusion, and the frightening events of their every day lives. These are their true paranormal stories.

Fowler Lake.

Ghostly Feelings

Sunday, June 24, 2007 16:45:28
From: Gail, Rockton, IL

I am very sensitive to psychic activity. I become light headed and dizzy with vertigo. My husband surprised me with an anniversary trip to the Inn at Pine Terrace on Fowler Lake this past weekend and we stayed in the tower room. From the second I entered our room I experienced all of my "ghosty" feelings, and they persisted throughout our stay. The feeling diminished in the hallway and got fainter as I moved downstairs. I knew, before I even did any research, that something was going on there. Thankfully, my husband doesn't think I'm insane! ;) Just thought you'd be interested.

Investigator Comments:

This is a very interesting story. We have heard other reports of paranormal activity at the Inn at Pine Terrace on Fowler Lake. We contacted the current owners and asked about the reported activity. They didn't have too much to say besides they had heard the stories but had not experienced anything strange themselves. We would love to investigate this location and take a look at the environment. Variations in the electromagnetic field (EMF) and ion levels can result in light-headedness and dizziness. We've had people in our group report the same symptoms when exposed to varying EMFs and ion counts. This doesn't mean that what was experienced isn't paranormal, it's just something that needs to be checked. Also, there are plenty of situations where unexplained EMF and ion changes are associated with paranormal activity. It would be good to compare the tower room to other locations where she had no experiences. Hopefully we will get the chance to investigate this location in the future.

Oak Hill Cemetery in Janesville, Wisconsin.

Lady in White at Oak Hill Cemetery

Sunday, June 18, 2006 10:28 AM
From: Carlos, Janesville, WI

Hello. I was wondering if you had heard of the Lady in White at Oak Hill Cemetery in Janesville, WI? I heard this place is haunted and people have had various experiences like seeing a lady in white floating through the cemetery, people seeing a greenish mist floating through the cemetery, voices talking to people when no one is there and screams. I was very intrigued by these stories and because I don't live to far away I thought I would do a little investigating at this location and see what I could find.

I got a few friends together and we took some cameras, video cameras, digital recorders, thermometers and radio shack hack and and EMF meter. We did our first investigation during the day so we could get a good feel for the place and would be able to see where we were going and what we were doing. I also don't mind investigating during the day cause I think paranormal activity can happen during the day or night and it doesn't happen just a night. Even though it is more fun and creepier during the night you have to investigate when the activity is said to happen. So, doing our first outing during the day didn't seem like a bad idea.

We pulled into the cemetery and drove around for a bit so we could pick a few good spots to investigate. We decided to focus on three areas – chapel, veterans area and the oldest part of the cemetery. We decided on these areas cause this is where we heard most of the reports of paranormal activity occurred and they looked the most interesting.

We parked the car, grabbed our equipment and started investigating. We took temperature readings, recorded video and checked the EMFs in the area. There were a few spots around the chapel where the temperature dropped about 10 degrees and then went back to normal when we moved out of that area. There were no changes in the EMF that we noticed. No other interesting readings were found in any of the areas.

Next we decided to do some EVP recordings. We sat by the Tallman grave (of the Lincoln Tallman House – and have you heard of this being haunted?). We settled in, got comfortable and started the recorders. We asked questions for about 15 mins and then stopped. I was eager to listen to the recording we had just done so I went to the car and grabbed some headphones. I listened intently to the recording and I think we captured something. It sounded like a woman's voice asking, "Where am I?" This was a very exciting finding cause we were pretty sure we didn't hear anyone say anything during the time of the recording session. We were pumped and ready to keep investigating.

We continued to walk through the cemetery and taking various readings. All of a sudden the EMF meter went from 0.5 to 10. At the same time it did this I felt a cold chill all around me. I had one of the other people check the temperature and there wasn't any drop in the temperature. Weird. It was pretty cold and I thought for sure there would have been a drop in temperature. After searching the area extensively we could find to reason or source for the EMF spike. After about a minute it went away. That was pretty interesting. After about another hour it was getting dark so we packed everything up and headed out.

We decided to return the next day to further investigate and hopefully repeat the findings we had the day before. As we were pulling into the cemetery one of my friends yelled, "STOP!!!" "LOOK!!!!" They pointed off to the right and we all looked over there. I didn't see anything but my friend thought for sure they had seen a lady in a white wedding dress walk between a few gravestones! We quickly drove over to the location where they thought they had seen the lady. We grabbed our equipment and scrambled out of the car and immediately started taking readings in the area. We got nothing on any of the equipment. I was really expecting and hoping that something would have turned up on the equipment since my friend saw something. This is someone I totally trust and when they said they saw something I believed them 100%.

Even though we didn't get any equipment readings and there were no other experiences that day we felt like it was a great trip.

Just wanted to share this story with you.

Investigator Comments:

We have heard various stories about the Lady in White and other paranormal activity at Oak Hill Cemetery in Janesville. We are not really sure what the source of this activity may be. But one needs to keep in mind that reports of Ladies in White are very common throughout the world. We do know that someone did commit suicide at the cemetery. We also know that Oak Hill was not the original cemetery in Janesville. The original cemetery was in the middle of courthouse hill at what is now known as Jefferson Park. This is where the first settlers buried their dead. Then in the 1850s the bodies were moved (at least most of them) to Oak Hill Cemetery to make way for the first high school to be built at the location. Perhaps the Lady in White is someone who was buried at the original cemetery and her body was moved and her spirit is trying to find her body.

Gravesite of loving husband greatly missed.

Church Graveyard Experience

Thursday, June 10, 2010 1:16AM
From: Jonathan, Clinton, WI

I wanted to let you all know about a paranormal experience I had when I was in Annapolis Maryland. It was one of the first truly paranormal experiences I have ever had and I wanted to share it with you all.

I was in Annapolis Maryland in late January for a meeting for work. The meeting got done early one afternoon so I decided to go for a walk with another person I worked with. We left the hotel and began our exploration of lovely historic Annapolis. The city was beautiful with the older buildings. It felt as if we had taken a step back into time. It was bitterly cold but I look forward to the walk through the streets to see the sights.

After walking a few blocks we approached a church in the middle of the city. It was definitely an older church. The thing that really caught our attention was a cemetery located on church property. I had never seen anything like this before – a church with a cemetery right in the middle of the town. A little exploration and I learned that this was St. Anne's Church and was first built in 1696. Talking about historic! I was thrilled to have found this location and wanted to explore further.

I asked the person I was with if he wanted to walk around the church and explore the cemetery. Since he was also interested in history he thought it would be fun. So, we entered the church grounds and began walking thru the cemetery. From the first moment that we entered the location, I felt like something was there with us...watching us...following us... It was like we were in an area where someone or something didn't want us to be. But not to be one to be scared or take those feelings seriously, I proceeded on thru the cold and admired the historic church and the old gravestones. It was no more than a few minutes later when something very strange had happened.

We were walking back and forth thru the cemetery when all of a sudden I smelled the very powerful scent of lilacs! I looked at the person I was with and without saying one word to him he asked, "Do you smell lilacs?' I responded with a positive head nod. We walked around the area to define exactly where the lilac scent was and to determine where it was coming from.

We could only smell the lilacs in a small 10 foot by10 foot area around a certain tombstone. We noted that none of the windows of the church were open so it could not have been coming from the church. We also looked over all the other graves and could not find any evidence of fresh lilacs. We were mystified on where the smell was coming from. It was January and freezing cold out and there were no fresh lilac anywhere to be found. After a little further searching we decided to make note of where the spot was and come back in five to ten minutes.

We walked over to the other side of the church and looked around for a bit. After five or ten minutes we headed back to where we smelled the lilacs. We approached the grave where we first smelled the lilacs. We were really expecting to again smell the fragrant flowers. But to our surprise there was nothing there! We walked around the entire area breathing in deeply thru our noses but did not smell the sweet scent of lilacs. We were greatly confused and wondered where the lilac smell had come from and where it had gone. It was at this point that we were starting to wonder if we would be able to find a natural explanation and source for the lilacs smell. We looked for the source a little longer but just couldn't find it! It was at this point that we thought we might be having a paranormal experience. We discussed it over and over and tried to come up with a natural explanation. After talking things over for a bit more we couldn't find a natural explanation! We were both thrilled and amazed that we just had a paranormal experience!

When I returned home from my trip I decided to look into St. Anne's Church and Cemetery. I was shocked to find that other people had reported experiences while in the cemetery! This was really exciting for me because I had not known anything about the location prior to my visit and experience. Then to find out other people had experiences there after the fact only led more excitement to my experience.

I thought you would like to know about this truly amazing experience! Best of luck in your search for life after death!

Investigator Comments:

WOW! This is a fascinating story. It is interesting that both people smelled the lilacs at the same time and same location in the middle of winter. The power of smell cannot be underestimated. Strange smells with no apparent natural explanation are commonly reported in locations with a history of paranormal activity. They are reported more frequently than visual apparitions. It would be good to know the details of what else they saw at this location. Why? Well the context can be very important. For example, if there was something purple that they both saw (even subconsciously), that might explain why they thought they smelled lilacs. It is interesting that they knew nothing about the location and only later found out there had been other experiences. This is the type of story that really makes one think there are some things that just can't be explained. Two people, similar experience, no prior knowledge of the activity at the location...makes one wonder...

Suspender Ghost

Tuesday, February 6, 2007, 6:17 AM
From: Amanda, Milwaukee, WI

I work in the Third Ward. There have been stories from people in our building and next door. Our graphic designer says she sees a man in a blue sweater and suspenders walking through the office at the end of the day. My experience is different. At the time this happen there were only 3 people in the office. Me and my 2 bosses. One of my bosse was sitting at my desk. I could see him clearly. As you walked down the hall you can see the stock room at the other end of the office. It is covered by a curtian. A goldish color. If the light is on you can usually see if anyone is in there. As I walked down the hall I saw a tall figure. Head and shoulders, tall. My other boss is tall so i thought it was her. As I approched the curtain I can see the figure moving. I pulled the curtian back asking a question of my boss. There was no one there. I turned in confusion and saw my boss sitting at her desk on the oppiste side of the office. Other stories of the building come from the printer next door. He has been in the office building for moe than 20 years I beleive. It was after closing of the day. He and one of his emplyees were in the warehouse that is directly attached to the offce. The front door was closed and locked. They both heard, very clearly, someone say “Hello”. They both looked at one another and asked “Didnt we lock the door?”, they went to look and no one was there. There are many more stories from people that have been in the Third Ward for years. I also was kicked on the leg from under my desk when I took at new position in the company. The person that use to hold this position had said serveral times she felt something rubbing her leg. I forgot about that until I was kicked. I was reminded of it by our graphic desinger that the previous sales person had the smae experience.

I have many more stories over the years that have happend to me when I lived in California as well. One in particular stands out. When my father-in-law dies. He had been hospitalized for weeks in a coma. He woke up one day and was aleart. That night I was awaken by my waterbed moving. There he was standing at the foot of my bed saying “Everything is ok now”. 30 seconds later the phone rang. The hospital calling to let me know he had died. Well that is all I have for now.

Investigator Comments:

Two comments on this email:

1. It is common to not realize you are seeing a ghost until after the experience happens and one later finds out there was not a living person there. The part where she thought it was her boss, but later found out is wasn't, fits this common ghostly experience perfectly.

2. The second part of this email that caught our attention was about the father-in-law dying. There are many reports of people having a loved one visit them at the time of death or shortly after they have died. These are known as crisis apparitions or apparitions of the dying. These experiences occur between two people with some type of emotional attachment. The person who passed away is just coming by to let their loved one know that everything is okay and they are moving on.

Paradise Road in Jefferson, Wisconsin.

Paradise Road

Sunday, October 30, 2005, 7:32 AM
From: Troy, Jefferson, WI

Im not sure if this falls under the kind of thing you guys would investigate but I feel it definetly needs some kind of attention. Paradise road outside of Jefferson has been written about in Weird Wisconsin and several reports have been found on forums and the like, but mostly just kids who had went out there for the thrill and come back with strange stories.

My friend and I decided to go out there and see if there really is something to the stories of a winged creature with glowing red eyes, inhuman screams, ghostly figures etc. as we live just down the highway some apartments in Jefferson and if something like this was nearby, we wanted to know more about it.

My friend is what some would call a "Sensative", she picks up on messages from the dead or other engergies, has short premonitions and is generally more sensative to another world we cant see. She had been particularly curious after hearing about Paradise road and wanted to go down there and see if she could pick up on anyone or anything (as she has not really had any training or anything to advance her skill and is somewhat cautious about letting anything about her ability be known, she does like to go out and try things occationally to see if she can find anything).

Well we went down there, we didnt have anything but a camera and our car, but before we even got far down the road my friend's breathing became very heavy and she got very quiet. She knew there was something VERY negative in the area and all she could define it as was something not human. She did also pick up on an old man in the same area, the name James and the number 1881, but the other negative energy was well overpowering that. She explained to me she felt very drained in the area, like there was some sort of vortex sucking her energy, something maintained by this other negative energy, and it made her very tired. After prodding for more details the best way she could describe this inhuman energy was as something like a chupacabra, gollum, or demon...somethng with red eyes, crouching and ready to pounce, maybe with large wings or something from the back, very old, and something that stays in the general area, but VERY negative and dangerous. She got the feeling that this thing was very responsible for the happenings in the area, and it seemed to jive with some of the reports. So in the end, i was afraid for her safety and we turned around before even getting to the woods that most people have their experiences in. We are both VERY curious what is out there but know that it is dangerous and cannot do it on our own or with our abilities. I just wanted to send this along as it seems to us to be something very old and very serious that no one talks about and needs to be addressed or investigated, as there were a few houses on that road and im sure these people have seen or heard things. The road is right off highway 18 on the right as you are heading out of Jefferson, past St. Coletta (another place my friend got many strange feelings from). Thankyou for taking the time to read through my report and hopefully this is worth looking into.

Thank you!

Investigator Comments:

There are many stories about Paradise Road. The vast majority of the reports come from high school kids looking for a thrill or trying to scare their girlfriends. However, the vast number of reports from this area does make it interesting. We have recently visited this location to look around and see what we could find. We drove around for awhile and stopped at a few locations. We didn't see anything out of the ordinary, nor did we have any experiences. However, we can certainly understand why this place would seem scary and foreboding at night. The comment about the chupacabra is interesting in itself as there have been many reports of a werewolf looking creature in southern Wisconsin known as the "Beast of Bray Road." Perhaps there is some common link between ghostly activity and other strange paranormal activity.

Turner Hall Ghost

Sunday, February 4, 2007, 12:47 PM
From: Sheila, Monroe, WI

Hello! I would like to tell you about The Turner Hall of Monroe in Monroe Wisconsin. The original Hall was built in 1868 and burned to the ground in 1936. Todays Hall was built on top of the old site and inlcudes some of the stone walls from the original building. I personally do not seem to be sensitive to possible presences. But I can say I have been in the hall alone many times closing up and have heard things such as the glass door to the restaurant opening and closing. Since I was the only one inside and I had already locked the outside doors I think it only resonable that upon hearing a definite opening and closing of that door while I was only across the room from it I should have been looking right at the person who entered. Noone was there. I know this seems like nothing, but I now have a young lady who works hear who was doing cleaning work after closing buy herself. She has told me she has seen two ghosts or presences in the room. One man and One woman but not together. She can still explain exactly where they were and what they were wearing. We have sort of a mini museum in our restaurant with quite a few pictures on the wall. Just out of curiosity I sad why don't you see if you can find them in the pictures anywhere. She was able to point right at a man in a picture and say definately he is who she saw. She has not yet found the woman however I don't think she has really looked over all the pictures yet. The man she pointed out has definatley passed on some time ago. I have no reason to believe she has lied or made anything up. She has also told me of seeing a female presence in a house she used to live in. I think the fact that she pointed him out on a picture to me is almost amazing. She never seems bothered or upset or scared at these things, She says hey! if they were going to hurt me they could have very easily. Other people have mentioned strange things in the building but no bad or harmful things. I kind of wish I could see what she saw but I don't know that I ever will. Just thought this would be of interest to you since she actually found a picture of the spirit she saw. Maybe you can join us for dinner some evening. See you then.

Investigator Comments:

This location seems promising since someone with no psychic ability is having experiences and it is in a location with a history of paranormal activity. And speaking of history, the fact that the girl was able to pick the person she saw from a photo speaks to the historical context of the situation. Being able to link past people to the history of a haunted location will bring more credibility to the reports of paranormal activity.

Poltergeist Activity

Wednesday, January 3, 2007, 12:22 AM
From: PJ, Manitowoc, WI

I have lived in this house for about two years. Before I bought the house it had a long history as a rental property. When I first moved in, I had some "poltergeist" like activity, such as garbage can lids flying off of the garbage can and landing across the room, windows that were propped open with a piece of heavy wood being unexpectedly closed, lights turned on/off, etc. I also heard footsteps in the kitchen and living room late at night after going to bed. Many of these events were witnessed by my fiancee.

At that time, I felt that whatever may be involved was more mischievous than malicious and that it was upset that I was in the process of updating and remodeling my house.I am engaged to be married and my fiancee and daughter now live with me. Over the course of the past year, her daughter has been awakened in the night by "shadows" that are sometimes silent, sometimes speak (i.e. "You have to get out, there's a fire (tonight after midnight, 1/3/2006)", and sometimes scream at her "like a dinosaur". She is three years old. When I walked into her room tonight I immediately had goose bumps on my arms and neck and noticed a cold area near her bed. I have had the same sensation previously in other areas of the house. In fact, I have been so upset by whatever "it" is that I have taunted it and commanded it to "show itself". But, obviously to no avail. In the bedroom across the hall (now my office) that she was in for about eight months, she described the occasional nighttime visitor as "The Crabman", but would not talk any more about it, other than to say that he would sometimes keep her awake while she was trying to go to sleep. All she would tell me is that it was a "tall man" and that it was "human". I don't think most three year-olds would describe a "shadow" this way.

Her 5 year-old brother stays here every other weekend and has not reported any abnormal events. Until my fiancee and daughter moved in, the paranormal events were mainly confined to the first floor kitchen and living room.

I have had a dog since January, 2006. On a number of occasions he has acted abnormally. This normally occurs in the kitchen and living room. He seems to want to greet a person that I cannot see. His tail wags and he seems excited, as if someone is there. On other occasions, he will look into the living room or the corner of the kitchen and start growling and barking and I have a hard time calming him down.

If you would be interested in conducting an investigation at my property, please contact me. I am interested only in truth and understand that you will conduct a scientific study of the phenomena that I described. I prefer to remain an anonymous client due to the small community that I live in and the professional position that I hold in it.

Thank You, PJ

Investigator Comments:

It's hard to determine what exactly is going on here, but a brief review of the different types of ghosts and hauntings would be appropriate. The first is known as a residual haunting or what some people call, "place memory." It is a moment in time that is somehow recorded in the environment. The event recorded is highly emotional in nature, either good or bad. Then under the right conditions and with the right person, the event replays itself. It is like a video loop playing over and over. There is no interaction between the living and the phenomenon. The second is the true "dead-guy" apparitions. This is the part of the human consciousness that survives bodily death. It displays intelligence and interacts with the people witnessing it. The third is poltergeist activity or what is termed, Recurrent Spontaneous Psychokinesis, "RSPK." It has nothing to do with a ghost or dead guy. It involves a living person known as the agent. This person is under some sort of stress and is releasing the stress subconsciously by affecting things in the environment. The object affected in the environment is symbolic to the things causing the stress. It is impossible to determine what is going on based on the information provided. It could be one thing or a combination of things. In order to appropriately address a situation, it is paramount to know what type of activity we might be dealing with.

Ghostly Footsteps

Wednesday, January 12, 2007, 2:52 PM
From: Dexter, New Berlin, WI

Hello. I wanted to share a story with you that I heard. It is about a house where the door would open every night at a certain time and then people would hear footsteps. Here ya go....

I was sitting around with a bunch of family members one holiday and we somehow got on the topic of ghosts. It seemed like once I brought up the topic everyone had some sort of story they could share with the family. However, there was one story that I found particularly interesting.

One of my family members told me that when they were a kid they used to live in a house in Illinois and something strange would happen every night. It was an old farmhouse and they had lived there for some time and there was really no history of anyone dying there. Even though they didn't know about anyone dying there they thought something strange must have happened at one point because of the weird things that happened.

As the family sat at the kitchen table around 7 to 8pm every night for dinner they would have the following happen...The back screen door would open by itself and that would grab everyone's attention. Then the door would close and they would hear footsteps walk across the kitchen floor right by where they were sitting. They were totally freaked out. The parents knew it was happening but would downplay it by saying it was just a draft or breeze from outside. Maybe that would explain the door opening and closing but how would that explain the footsteps? And why would it happen every night?
After the footsteps went by them in the kitchen they would hear them go down the hallway and then head towards the stairs. The footsteps would pause briefly and then they would continue up the stairs. It was one step at a time and it sounded pretty heavy... thud...thud..thud...thud....Until it reached the top of the stairs. They would then pause again for a brief moment. They would continue down the second floor hallway and then just stop!

Pretty crazy story! They said nothing else strange ever happened in that house. Just the door and footsteps.

I would have loved to visit this house but it is no longer in the family. I will try to contact the people who live there now and see if they report anything happening.

I would think this would be just the type of place that should be investigated. I mean people say you can't prove this stuff is real because it isn't repeatable. This seems pretty repeatable to me! How would people who don't believe explain seeing the door and hearing the footsteps every night at a certain time? This would be the type of proof that is needed to prove that there is life after death. I mean the scientists could study it all the time and try to figure out what is going on.

I would love to stay at a place like this and experience something really cool like that!!! Anyway, just thought you would like to hear about this

Investigator Comments:

Based on the information in the comments for the last email, this would seem to be a residual haunting.

Renovating Ghosts

Wednesday, September 1, 2004, 9:58 PM
From: Rick, Janesville, WI

For a period of time in late 1997 through 1999 i was employed in a building located in downtown janesville. at this time the business was occupied by All You Can Ink Tattoo. I was required to stay over night many times to work on the plumbing, painting, and other basic renovations. During this time, and throughout the ensuing years, I experienced several horrfying experiences that I will never forget.

The building is very old, as you know, I do not know much of the history but I do know that it used to be a shoe store at one point. When we tore out the walls in the lobby there were indvidual slots for displaying shoes running the length of each wall.

I spent a great deal of time building tattoo needles in the basement, and did not experience anything unusual, nor did i experience any feelings of dread or forboding that usually accompanied an encounter. I spent many nights sleeping in the main lobby, and each time it was a horrifying experience. Often I would wake up feeling as if someone were standing over me, or watching me. Once, after business hours, the floor manager and I were sitting at the desk on the first floor and we heard a sound that can only be described as a car being driven through the second floor wall. It literally scared the hell out of us, and we could never find a source of the noise, nor any physical or structual damage to the building itself.

The third floor is where i experienced the most personal activity. The building is now currently occupied by another business, which sells products on the main floor, and on the second floor. At the time of my encounters the second floor was divided into three tattoo stations. I would often play loud music while cleaning and mopping in the mornings. We had large five gallon jugs of Green Soap sitting on shelves in the third tattoo station. For some reason unknown to all of us, the jugs would always end up on the floor, or fall off on their own out of nowhere.

This was such a common occurance that we had to physically bind them to the shelf with large plastic ties. One morning during my routine cleaning I was in the third tattoo station and I left the room for less than 10 seconds, when I returned one of the jugs was on the floor, I did not hear it fall, or any other noise come from the room during my absence.

Once, I was in the middle tattoo station when I suddenly got the chills, and I felt hot breath on the back of my neck and someone whispered my name into my right ear. I turned around and of course, I was totally alone.

Nearly every week I would be on the third floor and hear loud party noises coming from the first floor. Clinking glasses, music, voices and laughter. I would walk to the edge of the stairs and look down to find it totally dark, and no one there. Many occuances happened to me, and other employees during the years, but these are the instances that stick out the most. The building is currently occupied by a different business, I believe the owner, not the employees, would be more receptive to questions, or any future investigations.

Investigator Comments:

This place is actually a location that we visit on our Janesville Haunted History Tour. On several occasions we have spoke to the employees of this location and they have plenty to say about it. They have all experienced, at one time or another, instances that they think were paranormal in nature. They have told us numerous stories of things that have happened to them while working. None of them want to go upstairs at the end of the night to shut the lights off. I can't say I blame them, with the history of experiences reported from this place. We would love the opportunity to get in and do a complete investigation sometime.

Creepy concrete crawl space.

Haunted Dream House

Thursday, March 16, 2006, 3:08 PM
From: Jacqui, Belvidere, IL

We had moved Into our dream house, we were just renting it at the time but we were going to buy it when the owner was ready to sell. We moved in on March 1st 2000. We were settled in and life there was very good.

The house had a partial basement and then a cement crawl space. My oldest son, he was 16 at the time, started to investigate the crawl space around April. He said it was very strange in there and he felt very uncomfortable when he was in there like he was being watched. One night in late April my second son, he was 1 1/2 at the time, started screaming in the middle of the night. I ran in to him to find him standing in his crib screaming at the corner of his room. It took me about an hour to calm him down. He did this several nights a week and I began to notice a watched feeling in our main bathroom. We had a very large sunken tub in this bathroom and there was a cement support for it in the crawl space. Everytime I was in the bathroom I would feel like someone was in there with me. I felt it to be a little boy, only not quite.

One night I awoke to find a little boy standing by my bed, he was transparent and when I said what's wrong to him he opened his mouth and groweled at me. His teeth we very pointed and he was not really a little boy. Then he disapeared. This upset me and I woke up my husband and we checked on the kids but they were okay. I was pregnant with out third son at this time, about 7 months and several nights after the sighting I was asleep, I had a dream that some type of blob was on my chest, holding down my arms and trying to cover my face. It did not seem to have any pressure on the baby though. I awoke to find that this presence was still there and I could not move. I thrashed my head back and forth so that it could not cover my face and I yelled for my husband and he woke up and it was gone. I would say it lasted about 45 seconds.

This scared me a great deal. I checked on the kids again, once again they were fine. I was so uncomfortable by this time that I would not sleep with the lights off, feeling something looming over me everytime I turned them off. Even a night light wasn't enough. The presence would call my name when I was laying in bed and it was very unnerving for me because the voice sounded, I don't really know how to explain it, evil maybe. That isn't quite right but it did scare the hell out of me. Finally, I told my husband that I just couldn't stay there any more. I was causing trauma for myself and my children. So we moved to a different house that I am happy to report is clear of that kind of evil. i have always wanted to research the house, I did love it so much, I'm just not sure how to go about it. Now it is for sale and I am afraid that whoever buys it will tear it down and build a business there. It is located on commercial property and I think it is destined to go down.

Investigator Comments:

This would be another location where we would love to examine the environment. The electromagnetic fields in the crawl space and bathroom could be interesting. The stress and hormonal changes associated with the pregnancy could also be playing a role. The episode when she was sleeping could have been old hag syndrome with associated sleep paralysis. These are just a few possible natural explanations. Of course the house could have just harbored some sort of paranormal activity. The good thing is that nothing happened after they moved. Maybe we will hear from the new owners of this house.

Renaissance Faire Ghosts

Friday, April 18, 2003, 4:19 PM
From: Edith, Edgerton, WI

I have always loved ghost stories-having grown up in a house where "things" happened and being quite sensitive to spirits- but when I bartended full time one of my favorite Halloween activities would be to ask customers to tell me their favorite true ghost story. The man that told me this is a manager. He told me this story when I worked in Il.

If you follow the frontage road going S. from Bristol WI toward Illinois-the one that is parellel to route 41-near the Renaissance Faire-this is where the story takes place.

This man told me he was driving home from a friends on a Friday evening late, but sober and suddendly he looks up to see a woman in the road. At this point it is too late for him to slow down and he braces himself for the impact---but drives right through her instead. So he is shaken up and several days later relates this story to a friend that tells him a similar story-except that he swerved to avoid hitting her and his car skidded into the cemetary.

I have not had time to check this place out---but does anyone have any more info about this? Also do you ever need "sensitive" people to assist in your investigations?

Thanks.

Investigator Comments:

This sounds like a case of the traditional phantom hitch hiker. There are stories from all over the world where people report seeing a woman walking down the street. Sometimes they stop and pick them up only to have them disappear from their car and other times they mysteriously drive through them. The areas where these are experienced usually are associated with a tragedy. Unfortunately, we don't have any specific information about this area.

Underground Railroad Ghosts

Thursday, March 30, 2006, 2:27 PM
From: Robert, Janesville, WI

Well, according to what I have been told, this building used to be a part of the underground railroad. It has a tunnel that goes underneath the street... I don't know the history of the building yet, as I am researching it. But strange things happen here once in a while... Like things will be in a totally different place then where you left them, lights will go on and off by themselves sometimes. Strange noises have been heard by the employees, footsteps have been heard on several occasions coming up the stairs to the office, but then no one is there... Voices coming from the back room have been heard, children's laughter sometimes... They are harmless to us, but there presence is known to the employees and residents of this building. I personally would like to investigate this phenomenon, but the owner of the building insists he doesn't want to disturb them. I have begun my own investigation and will post my findings if you wish...

Investigator Comments:

We look forward to seeing what they find during their investigation. There are many ghost stories associated with buildings on the underground railroad. Two other locations in Wisconsin include the Octagon House in Fond du lac and the Milton House in Milton.

The Weeping Girl

Tuesday, February 6, 2007, 6:17 AM
From: Johnny, Burlington, WI

On the way we were talking about things and all of a sudden I got this feeling, I got really anxious and the hair on the back of my neck was on end, (im bald so this is quite a feat)

I asked him if anything happened on around where we were at and he told me about a girl dieing in an aout accident around janurary, we got a little further down the road and I all of a sudden got this cold heavy feeling in my chest and started to cry, I have never felt the kind of sadness I did then.

By the time we got to burlington most of the feeling had went away but I still felt something there. I do not know who the girl was but I do know she is very sad. this only happened last night and it was my first time driving down that road, so I dont know if it will ever happen again, he also told me that there was a cross there in her memory.

I hope that helps.

Investigator Comments:

Sounds like a little extra sensory perception was used to pick up on the accident and the girl that died. Even if the cross was perceived subconsciously, the flood of emotion was remarkable. We would be interested in knowing if this has happened to them anywhere else.

Ohio State Reformatory

Sunday, December 26, 2010, 2:40 AM
From: David, Janesville, WI

I wanted to tell you about a really interesting paranormal experience that I had while at the Ohio State Reformatory.

I went on a group ghost hunt with some paranormal investigators. We took a bus and it took about six hours to get there. As the bus pulled up to OSR I was completely amazed by how large the structure was and how spooky it looked. If there was ever a place to be haunted this would be it!

We exited the bus and entered the newer reception office area. The people who run OSR introduced themselves and told us a bit about the history of the location. After the brief overview it was time for a guided tour.

We walked thru the entire prison - the six tiers of free standing jail cells, solitary confinement, the guard towers, chapel, shower area, hospital and the warden's living quarters. Walking thru the building was an amazing experience. To see the old jail cells which still had the beds and toilets in the cell was just plain creepy! The place was incredible...and to think about all the people who were prisoners there and all those who had died made the experience almost overwhelming. I was looking forward to investigating the location!

I wasn't sure what to expect for the investigation but I soon found out that we could pretty much go and do whatever we wanted to for the entire evening. Then the lights were shut off and we were free to roam on our own.

I wondered thru the prison by myself and sometimes with other people. It was amazing to walk thru solitary confinement all by myself in complete darkness. A little scary but exhilarating!

I continued to explore the various areas of the prison and they were all dark and creepy. It was unbelievable that I didn't see more than a few other people the entire night even though about 100 had gone on the trip.

About half way thru the night it was time for pizza and soda. After the break I headed out with three people to explore the warden's quarters. This was like a large mansion within the prison. I found it simply amazing that the warden and his family would live right there at the prison. Seems like that would be a unique kind of family life to say the least!!!

We slowly explored the entire warden's quarters – going from one floor to the next with only our flashlights to lead us thru the darkness.

We then went up a set of stairs and came around a corner. As soon as we turned the corner I smelled roses! I turned to the other people I was with and asked them if they smelled roses? They all said yes.

Smelling roses is NOT something one would expect to smell at OSR. It was a old somewhat run down facility and it mostly smelled like an old nasty boys locker room…damp and nasty!

We tried to determine where the rose smell was coming from but it seemed to be moving up and down the hallway. As we were walking down the hallway another group of about 10 people approached us and immediately asked if smelled roses. We said yes and we all continued looking for the source of the rose scent. After another 30 minutes or so we went back down to the meeting area and told people what we had experienced.

After a bit of discussion about what had happened and what we would do next it was decided that we would line people up and down the hallway where we experienced the rose smell. We also did some readings with the various equipment in the area but nothing was detected.

Once people were in place up and down the hallway, we waited. All of a sudden someone at the far end of the hallway said that they smelled roses. Then they said it was gone and within a few seconds the next person down said they smelled roses. People up and down the hallway reported smelling roses and then not smelling them. One person decide to again try to follow the rose scent and determine where it was coming from and where it was going. He followed it down the hallway into a room and then to a closet within that room…And then it was gone. No one else smelled it the entire night.

We found out that the hallway and room where it went to and disappeared was an area where one of the warden's wife's would spend a lot of time. We also found out that the closet and room was the location where Helen Bauer Glattke was accidentally shot when a handgun fell out of a box that was in the closet when she was trying to get a jewelry box out of the closet. Helen died three days later from pneumonia!

We thought this was pretty interesting since the rose scent did seem to be like that of rose perfume. We thought maybe the ghost of the warden's wife was still waking up and down the hallway and going to the closet to get her jewelry.

The fact that so many people had the same experience and it was in the area where the warden's wife used to walk around and where she was accidentally shot made this an extremely interesting experience.

Just wanted to share it with you!

Investigator Comments:

Great experience! Sounds like it could be a residual haunting where the route of the wardens wife while walking was embedded into the history of the building.

The Paulding Lights

Sunday, November 21, 2010, 5:22 PM
From: Gordon, Superior, WI

Hey there ghost hunting people...I wanted to tell you about an experience I while visiting Paulding, MI. Have you heard of this location? Have you been there? What do you think is going on at that location? Did you have any experiences when you were there? Cause I sure in the heck did. It was a really cool place and I stayed there for a few days and nights and every night I would go there and experience some sort of weird activity. I know a couple of ghost hunting groups and paranormal investigators have visited this location and I think unexplained mysteries was even there and they pretty much decided that it was unexplainable and something weird was going on there. I know some pople think it is nothing more than car lights and red car lights but I think there has to be something more going on there. Why? Cause I have seen it with my own eyes and I just cant explain it naturally at all. I have tried and tried but to no avail and I really tried and I think I thought of everything that it could have been naturally but none of the natural explainations explain what has been happeneing there. The first night I was there I went to the location and there was about 100 people there. Pretty amazing and I wasn't to thrilled with all those people there cause I wasn't sure anything would happen with all those people disturbing the paranormal. I eventually worked my way to the front of the corwd cause I wanted a front row seat. I traveled a long way and didn't wanna miss anyting that was going to happen. I was watching very carefully and then all of a sudden there it was! A bright light off in the distance just abopve the skyline. It sat there and just hovered for a long time. It stayed there so long that there is no way it was a car passing somewhere cause the car would have just have to had sat there for a long time. The other thing was that it changed colors – red-white-red-white-blue and orange. Then it got brighter and closer. It was like coming right at the group of people. Some of the girls in the crowd were getting scared and wanted their boyfriends to leave. I don't think they left. Anyway eventually the light jus disappeared. As quick as it came it went away. That was pretty amazing. And that was just the first night of the paranormal at Paulding. I was totally excited and wanted to explore the area a little bit during the day so I could get a good feel for the location and what might possibility be going on at that location. I drove around most of the day the next day. I checked out pretty much everything within 5 to 10 miles of the spot. I drove way up the road to see if it could be cars but I didn't think it could be. I also drove on some dirt roads further down in the valley that you look over when you see the lights. I saw a few small home and some trailors but theye didnt seem to have nay lights that would look like what I saw the night before. I then went back to the top of the valley where I was last night. I parked the car and walked down into the big valley. It was a long walk and the light must have come from very far away. There was a stream to cross and it seemed very heavily forested. Lots of places where the paranormal could hide down there. Even with many people I am not sure if you would have been able to find them. You could definitely tell where the old road and railroad tracks were. I wanted to confirm the railroad tracks because one of the theries says that a railroad guy got killed on the tracks and he walks up and down the track with his lantern looking for his body. Or maybe he was looking for his head because he was decapitated. I will have to check on that story and get back to you. Another idea is that is just some other type of spook lights. Some people even claim it is UFOs. That could be. Because lots of UFO sightings have strange colored lights just like people have been experiencing when there. I also noticed there were lots of high powered electrical lines in the area. Maybe that is what the paranormals are feeding off of in order to manifest. That is a pretty well known fact in the paranormal community. So, the next night I went back out there to experience some more paranormal. I was not let down. As soon as I arrived the lights were back. This time they were different. They were red and blue and were getting real close. It looked like they were riding the power lines and going back and forth. The hair on my arms and the back of my neck was standing up when this activity was going on. It was really awesome to have paranormal so close to me. I was kinda scared but not enough to leave. I think I became more fascinated as the longer I was there. After awhile I thought of something... maybe it was swamp gas or something. So I smelled around the area but couldn't detect and weird smells that would make me think it was swamp gas. Then I though what was making it burn. So, I concluded it couldn't really be swamp gas. This place is a legitimate mystery and I think more scientific like people need to study it and find out what is going on here. This isn't the only place in the world that has these kinds of mysterious lights. So maybe people could study all these areas and really get to know and understand these paranormals. I hope this information helps you in your research of the unkown. I will get back to you after I visit the location again with my findings.

Investigator Comments:

Yes, we have been there and did see the lights. It sounds like this person has thought of all the possibilities. We look forward to hearing about their future visits.

Missing Guest at My Hotel

Wednesday, December 29, 2010, 3:20 PM
From: Noah, Janesville, WI

Tim's parents bought a hotel after the owners died unexpectedly. It was an old looking hotel. Some people did not like Tim's parents business. Mr. Bush is a hotel owner right across the street from Tim's parent's hotel and Mrs. Wayne is the person in town. She wants to buy the hotel from Tim's parents and build a fashion shop. Tim's parents spent their life savings remodeling the hotel. When it was done, they moved in and started their business. Time loved to swim in the pool and prank the guests. Mr. Smith and his wife checked in for a weeks stay. Tim especially enjoyed playing tricks on them because Mr. Smith screamed like a girl. On Wednesday, Tim snuck into their room, moved all of their things, and made a ghost out of his basketball and a white sheet. It would have been a good prank except that they never returned to their room.

Curious, Tim asked his parents why the Smiths left early. His parents said, "Not again! That is the third couple this week!" "Did they leave all of their stuff too?" asked dad. "Yes" said Tim, "and they did not check out either." While walking around in the hotel, Tim heard a guest talking about ghosts in the hotel. That made Tim decide to go ghost hunting. Armed with a flashlight, he went back into Mr. and Mrs. Smith's room. He screamed when he first went in, as he saw the ghost in the corner. He felt relieved when he realized it was just his basketball covered in a sheet. Tim was about to leave when he heard a ghostly voice say "change."

Scared, Tim ran back to his room and changed his underwear. Then he hid under his blankets. The next day he felt brave and went back to the room. But before Tim went in the room he heard his parents and Mr. Bush fighting over the hotel. Tim was sure he imagined the voices. Tim opened the door and found a couple sitting on the bed. At first Tim thought new guests had checked in, until he realized that he could see through them! At first Time as scared, but then he saw that they looked mad. Now Tim was really scared. "Why did the hotel change?" asked the man Tim could see through. "We will find out," said the woman. "I can tell you why the hotel changed," said Tim. Tim told them that they had died and that his parents had bought the hotel and redecorated. Hearing that they were dead, the ghosts got angrier. They told Tim that they would not return the missing guests until their hotel was back to the way it was. Then they disappeared.

Tim found the old decorations in the attic, and started to return the hotel to it's original state. His parents got mad and told him to put that old stuff away. This must have angered the ghost, because they turned the missing guests into ghosts! There were ghosts everywhere and they scared away the new guests.

Tim's parents know they had to do something or they would lose the hotel. They grabbed the old stuff and put the hotel the way that it was when they bought it. There was a flash of light and the ghosts vanished! The old guests came back and everything went back to normal. "Aaahhhh," Mr. Smith said when he got back in his room.

The End

Investigator Comments:

This is a great story on so many levels. It symbolizes the classic ghosts becoming active during renovations story that has been reported throughout the years. It also alludes to the idea that ghosts don't know that they are dead. The ghosts in this story had returned to the hotel that they had loved when they were alive. They were confused and angry that changes had been made. They had no idea that they were dead. Once the hotel was returned to its original state, then they were happy and left everyone alone and both the living and the dead coexisted peacefully.

Fireplace inside room where paranormal activity occurs.

Haunted Bed and Breakfast

Thursday, December 30, 2010, 6:03 AM
From: Dave, Janesville, WI

Hey Jen...I have gotten some e-mails in regards to the Antique Rose being haunted. Interesting because I had an experience there a few years back... Here's what happened to me...

I wanted to tell you about an experience I had at a Bed and Breakfast that is located in Janesville, Wisconsin. This happened a number of years ago and I wanted to tell you about it and find out if you have ever heard about this place.

It is called the Antique Rose and it is located in the Court House Hill Historic District in downtown Janesville, Wisconsin. As I pulled up to the Bed and Breakfast I was impressed by how loveliness of this antique Queen Ann Victorian. It seemed like a moment in time that had survived the many years in excellent condition. I was eager to get inside and see what this historic gem had in store. As I entered the Bed and Breakfast I was equally impressed with the inside as I was with the outside. It was very welcoming and I instantly felt at home. This is exactly how one should feel when staying at a Bed and Breakfast. The inside was absolutely beautiful. It was decorated appropriately for a historic Queen Ann Victorian. Appropriate but very functional and comfortable. I was ready to settle in for a little rest and relaxation after a long day at work and a long drive.

I made my way upstairs and made myself comfortable in my room. I read some of the brochures on the Janesville area and attractions and learned this area was rich in history and had an abundance of things to do to keep one occupied. I soon grew hungry and decided to venture out into the town for dinner. After an excellent meal I returned to the Antique Rose and was ready to settle in for a good nights rest. I went inside and noticed no one was in the house. I continued up to my room, unlocked my room and went inside. I was surprised to see that the bed covers were pulled back and there was a small piece of candy on my pillow. I thought that was a very nice touch! I soon heard the owners to return home and I thought I would go downstairs and thank them for pulling back the covers and leaving the candy. I went downstairs and thanked the owners for their hospitality in regards to the bed covers and the candy. They looked at me rather confused and said they had no idea what I was talking about. They said they had left at the same time I had and did not do anything in the room. Puzzled, I returned to my room. After doing a little reading I turned out the lights and got comfortable in bed. I soon fell asleep. A few hours later I woke up and was extremely hot and sweaty. It felt like it was about 100 degrees in the room. I got out of bed and looked around. To my surprise the room was rather cool. I went back over to the bed and noticed that the heating blanket was plugged in and turned to 'high.' Now I know I did NOT turn the blanket on and I actually remember it being unplugged when I went to bed. I checked to see if the bedroom door was locked and it was. So, I knew no one had entered the room and plugged in and turned on the blanket. I was beginning to wonder if this place had some paranormal activity. After laying awake in bed for awhile I soon drifted off to dream land. At about 4am I woke up. When I awoke I found that I couldn't move at all. I quickly learned that all the bed covers were tucked in very tightly around me! This was very strange as my arms were at my side and there was no way I could have done this to my self! I finally got out of bed and immediately looked around the room. No one was there and the door to my room was locked. I thought about the two strange experiences that I had and wondered if anyone else had experiences similar to these I couldn't go back to sleep so I sat in bed and read a book. Since I woke up at 4am I had this uneasy feeling that something was wrong. I had no idea what it was. So after a few hours of uneasy reading I got up, showered and went downstairs for breakfast.

I told the owners about my bedtime experience and they jokingly said, "maybe it was the ghost." Of course that immediately caught my attention and I asked them what they meant. They just shrugged it off and said it was just a joke. I'm not sure they were kidding around. I tried to discuss the issue further but it was obvious that they did not want to discuss it.

Breakfast was wonderful but I just couldn't eat much. My stomach was upset and I just didn't feel right. I thought maybe I was getting sick and that would explain my uneasy feeling that entire morning. I ate as much as I could and then went back upstairs to pack my bag and prepare to leave.

I grabbed my bag and took it down to my car. I checked my cell phone that was in the car and noticed I had missed a call from my parents. I immediately called them back and got some very sad news. My dad had informed me that my grandfather had passed away during the night. I was very upset at the news and felt as if I should have been there. I was planning a stop in Milwaukee after I finished up business in Janesville. I regretted not stopping to see my grandfather first before going to Janesville!

I wonder if my uneasy feeling was due to me somehow picking up on my grandfather's death? I also wonder if the events that happened that night in the bed and breakfast were due to my grandfather. I will never know for sure but regardless it was an interesting, emotional and sad time at the Antique Rose. I would love to visit the location again sometime and see if I have any experiences.

Investigator Comments:

What an interesting and touching story. This location is on the Janesville Haunted History Tour because of this story and the fact that other people have reported having experiences while staying at this location.

Chapter Four

Was There a Job Posting on Craigslist?

This chapter focuses on emails we received from people who are interested in becoming members or investigators with the Southern Wisconsin Paranormal Research Group. These are their email inquiries.

I Believe in the Supernatural!

Wednesday, October 22, 2003 11:07 PM
From: Candice, Janesville, WI

I'm interested in becoming a member. I love the supeernatural. I and my mother's family experience things. I need to get to the botttom of these experiences. Paranormal activity has happened in my mother's family for years, although the most of the ones who have experienced these phenomena are now dead. I do have my mother on tape telling the stories that I had heard personally from the people who experienced these things.

I have had many feelings as well as noises and sights. I have been in houses alone where strange noises and whispers have rushed by my ears. Also smells and strange feelings.

I believe in the supernatural. We need to find the truth.

Investigator Comments:

What's that line from *X-Files*? ... "The Truth is Out There." Keep looking!

Yes...I Am A Believer!

Tuesday, August 17, 2004 4:51 PM
From: Alex, Racine, WI

I'm very interested in seeking information and experiencing additional unexplained occcurances in the paranormal world. Yes...I am a believer!

Yes, but only on my own (not with any group or organization). I used to seek out old abandonned houses and farms, especially those rumoured to be "haunted". I have seen and experienced many things over the years, and have just recently taken my first photo of possible spirits in a local cemetery.

I believe I am more perseptive to things that others aren't. I have seen people after their death, shadows, experienced cold spots, apparitions, heard things that others could not hear. I write well and spend allot of time typing. I'm also working on becoming a minister. If there's a chance I can "clean house", so-to-speak, I am willing to try. Not as far as an exorcism, but more like house blessings.

Investigator Comments:

Question: Why would they want to join our group if they say, "Yes...I am a believer! Yes, but only on my own (not with any group or organization). And, "I write well and spend allot of time typing." Ummm, okay.

Huge Fan of the Paranormal Activities

Sunday, September 19, 2004 1:20 PM
From: Naomi, Bradford, WI

Hello, I was very much interested in this site u have going on here.. Actually I've never known Wisconsin had a paranormal group, guess u learn a little something cooler everyday.. Anywho, I've alwayz been a huge fan on the paranormal activities and such seein how I've grown up watchin more horror flicks of our famous yet great Micheal Myers than childh0od cartoons;my love for the craze and unknown alwayz heighted!

Getting the chance to understand those on earth mentally disturbed seeking someone to comprehend them and those in spirit seeking the same; i've alwayz been one in search of the unknown. Waiting, wanting to seek out whatz hidden so amazingly beneath our brow.:P .. The boggling craving knowledge of the unknown are yet to be discovered and I understand many wish to so badly to be seeked out by us humans since we are their final resort to puzzling pieces on earth...Long story short I would love to join your membership but i was also wondering what exactly is it that I must do to get into paranorml searching myself..Very much interested I am truly indeed...please contact me as soon as u can.. Thankyou, Greatly appreciated....Peace

Investigator Comments:

Wazz up...with this message? Anywho...as far as getting involved in paranormal research, we would suggest reading some books and journals in parapsychology, psychology, ghost hunting, metaphysics, physics, etc. Learn as much as you can and learn from a group who has been around for a while. Thanks...we will be in touch!

Experienced Psychic, Channeler & Healer

Sunday, September 18, 2005 7:07 PM
From: Devin, Onalaska, WI

I have been doing my own researching for a while now and its becoming over whelming to do it alone. I just did a full investigation for a residential haunting here in Onalaska. I have some equipment and I am ready to join a team and experience more.

Yes, I have a lot of experience. I think I can bring a lot. I own my own business. I am a psychic, channeler, healer etc..Please look at my website to get more of an idea of who I am. I am also clairvoyant, clairaudient, clairgustant etc. I have had special gifts and or abilities since I was very little.

Investigator Comments:

Who said it isn't good to work on your own? Sounds like you already got it covered!

Recent Paranormal Activity

Wednesday, October 2, 2005 9:17 AM
From: Karin, Milwaukee, WI

Hello, I am moving to the Milwaukee area in the next month from Florida and I have had very recently a paranormal experience at my families home in Houston, TX. I will explain at a later date what occored, but I am very interested in joining your group and helping any way I can while gaining more understanding of what had happened to me. I guess I want a better understanding of what the membership consists of and what you as a group do? Thanks and I hope to talk to you soon.

Investigator Comments:

We have two types of membership. Associate Members and Investigators. Associate Members can do everything Investigators do except go on private investigations. When a new Investigator is needed, we draw from the Associate Members. Our group researches, documents, and provides the best information possible on paranormal activity as it relates to ghosts and hauntings. The SWPRG is a science-based organization that collects data and seeks to understand paranormal phenomena based on what the data tells us.

Grew Up With All Kinds of Weird Happenings!

Wednesday, October 26, 2005 2:15 PM
From: Marsha, Dodgeville, WI

It was obvious from group websites who was and was not serious about what they were doing. I think "ghost hunting" in general tends to get a bad rap. I don't want to be part of something that adds to the stereotype. The impression I got from reading through your website is that this group is serious and professional.

I grew up in an old farmhouse built in the late 1800's with all kinds of weird happenings. (things being knocked over, falling off walls, lights turning off, phantom running water, feeling like i was being pushed, cold/ creepy feelings, and actually seeing a spirit, doors slamming etc.) I do try when I go places to visit known haunts. (queen mary, whitechapel in london)

I'm a good writer, I have experience with ghotsts, and I'm very eager and willing to learn.

Investigator Comments:

Eager and willing to learn are two of the most important characteristics we look for in new investigators. Yes, our group is serious and professional. When Investigating the Haunted, You should ALWAYS take Ghost Hunting to the Next Level!

Interested in Working with a Professional and Serious Team

Tuesday, Janaury 3, 2006 10:37 AM
From: Tim, Milwaukee, WI

While the science of paranormal research has come a long ways since using Ouija boards and candles, many people still think that "ghost hunters" are chasing their own shadows. I want to help make paranormal research more objective and, in turn, more credible to the scientific community. I have been interested in the paranormal since I was in grade school, but I have not had the opportunity to work with other people that want to take this work professionally and seriously.

My experience:

-I have a Bachelors of Science (Metallurgy)

-An excellent writer

-Open Minded

-Some people skills

-Well versed in Excel, Word, and data gathering.

-Familiar with most of the measuring devices used in investigations (per your website)

-A desire to explore and have fun

-A professional attitude

Investigator Comments:

Tim actually became a member of the SWPRG and worked with the group for a couple years. Tim is a great investigator, but like many others, his paranormal life unfortunately took a side seat to the ever-increasing demands of a serious and active paranormal investigator. Tim, you will be missed in this field. Hope you find time here and there at least to keep the spark alive. Ghost hunting groups need more investigators like Tim. People who can critically think and analyze situations. Not to mention the ability to construct a professional, well though out, researched, spell-checked and serious e-mail. Doing so makes us look more professional to our clients.

I Am Able to Contact The Dead

Tuesday, December 22, 2005 2:22 AM
From: Brian, Sister Bay, WI

I have my whole life been very intrigued by hauntings and ghosts, and just learning as much as I can about the dead. This seems like a good way of going about that. Also to be able to work with people who feel the same way as I do, Would be just exciting.

As a young child a friend and I would spend hours in cemetaries around California with tape recorders and video recorders trying to find any proff of ghosts or unnatural phenominas, Closest I got was actually not by any of these means. Infact the only times I was able to "contact" the dead was when I was younger. I was able to stand in one spot of my child hood home and hear seemingly hundreds of voices calling out my name.

I have spent a great majority of my life trying to find proff of exsistens of life after death, to contact the decessed. I amnot a great writer, I take many pictures, that sadly never turn out anything. Between the ages of I would say 7 (after my baby brother died) to the age of 14 I would hear crying, calls of my name, see figures move about my house. Never once was I scared or thought harmful things were going to happen. I have always been facinated by these occurances.

Investigator Comments:

We can understand how the loss of a baby brother can drive someone to want to understand the paranormal and determine if there is life after death. Especially with a variety of experiences before and after that tragic event. We hope they will find the answers they seek.

I Consider Myself Slightly "Psychic"

Sunday, January 29, 2006 6:44 PM
From: Debora, Fox Lake, WI

I'm very interested in what your group does and considering becoming a member. If at all possible I'd appreciate someone from your group contacting me, via e-mail or phone or whatever is available. I do believe I could be an asset to your group. However, still I'd like to learn more about your group before I commit to paying the membership fee.

A hopefully brief description of myself would be I'm 45 years old, married, and born and raised in southern Wisconsin. I've always been interested in "spirits", paranormal activity and the unknown, but haven't had much luck in finding people who are interested as well. I am Wiccan, not sure that matters, but I feel as though I should tell you because it pertains to the fact that I consider myself slightly "psychic" for lack of better word. That is what fuels my interest to the unkown. Ok enough for now. Thank you in advance if you decide to contact me. If not, I do appreciate what your group does and hope you continue to develope and grow and of course, learn.

Investigator Comments:

It seems like more and more people are interested in the paranormal everyday. We hope you find a group to explore your interests with and we appreciate your interest in the field.

Ex Witch and Satanist Looking to Join Your Group

Tuesday, November 22, 2005 4:58 PM
From: Dwayne, Walworth, WI

I want to joint the group because well i used to study witch craft and satanism and so i thought it might be a goos experience for me to go on expeditions of my own or with a small team here around my area. I have a picture that i took in my own home where i have accually caught my own ghost.I can only be an associate member for right now cause i dont really have the money right now that christmas is on its way and i have 3 step kids to buy for and my g/f(fiance) who loves to have money and its my dream to be apart of a team thats is un normal to other hobbies that people do and would ike to be recognized for the things that i do :)

i dont have much experience but i study all the time and i used to study witch craft and satanism (not kool i kow but it was fun for the moment)

well i do know of a few places here in Walworth that most people dont know about that are trully haunted. i know this cause i have lived here for 21 years and have accually witnessed these places haveing wierd un normal things happening to them.

Investigator Comments:

We would love to see the picture you took. Being an Associate Member is good because that is how we start all new members out when they first join the group. The one thing to caution you on is that hardly any serious paranormal researchers get recognized for the hard work that they do. Make sure you get into the field for your own knowledge and satisfaction otherwise you may be disappointed.

In Between a 3D and 2D World

Friday, June 23, 2006 7:30 PM
From: Devin, Egg Harbor, WI

i have always been interested in the field ,,i had a few things happen to me to prove there is a second and even thrird level of sprits with us ,i belive were in between a 3d world and a 2d world if that makes sence

i have done by myself ,,,evp,,and digital photos ,,

thats about it ,,

this may sound silly but i can sometimes feel if something is there or not ,,i love to take pics,,and vids,,i love the field ,,that helps

Investigator Comments:

Question: What happened to the first level spirits? Between a 3D and 2D world? Actually, we all live in a 4D world, so give us a ring when you get here.

Enthusiast of All Things Paranormal

Monday, October 23, 2006 8:33 AM
From: Jackie, LaCrosse, WI

I have been a long time enthusiast of all things paranormal. But I've always been a little dismayed by the overzealous approach that doesn't take the time to ask the skeptical questions. In recent years I've been seeing the scientific approach melding with paranormal investigation. (Yes, I'm a fan of the Sci-Fi Ghost Hunters show) This is the first I've heard of a group this close to LaCrosse that approaches the material in such a balanced scientific manner.

I could bring to your group an understanding of myth, legend and lore with an emphasis in Native American legends. A scientific analytical mind that will approach any matter in a skeptical manner first.

Investigator Comments:

It is great that the scientific approach is melding with the paranormal field. Unfortunately, this is not yet a common practice. The field certainly could use more scientific and analytical minds!

My Gift!

Sunday, November 12, 2006 12:31 PM
From: Edith, Fort Atkinson, WI

I would like to use my gifts as a psychic medium as i have not gone public with my gift.I have only used my gift online to help people connect to their loved ones who have passed on.

i am able to hear spirits who have crossed over but have never gone "ghost hunting"

I would like to bring my gift to the group!

Investigator Comments:

Online? World Wide Web? We think you've gone public. It sounds like you are using your gift in a positive way by helping people connect with their loved ones. Keep up the good work and we will be in touch if we need a psychic medium.

My Brain and Logic Determine My Actions and Reactions

Saturday, December 23, 2006 8:57 PM
From: Bristol, Germantown, WI

I want to join because I love the paranormal and I would love to be a part of a group that takes it as seriously as I do.

I have conducted small ghost hunts for people before but nothing on a huge scale

Not to brag, but I have a vas knowledge of the paranormal. I have conducted ghost hunts for people I knew from High School who felt that there was something in their homes that was paranormal. I ave 12 years of very deep interest in the paranormal to offer the group and I have spent so many hours of my life researching the paranormal in all of it's aspects. I also am a very down to earth person who does not lose her head when something scares me. I am not easily given In to emotion and my brain does the thinking for me. In situations where a ghost might be present, I keep very calm and take everything very seriously but use logic to determine what it may or may not have been. My brain and logic determine my actions and reactions (never overly scared or emotional) in investigations.

Investigator Comments:

It sounds like you have an excellent mind set and approach to the field. We never understood why people get into this field and then run away when they have a paranormal experience. Seems ridiculous and counterproductive.

I Know I Would Be Your Best Bet As A Fellow Investigator!

Tuesday, May 15, 2007 6:05 PM
From: Tammy, Rockford, IL

Looking for group in my area, (northern Illinois) very hard to find. I am interested in all things paranormal and have studied it over the years.

I have done amature hunting with friends (digital cams in cemeteries) and have gone on one investigation with NIGHT (northern illinois ghost hunting team) 2 years ago at the Villisca ax murder house in Iowa. Used night vision cams, digital recorders, temp gauges, digital cameras, lap top.

I have read Many, Many books on the paranormal, watch everything I can on it, and have a strong belief in the paranormal, but not tooo much to make every little noise freak me out, I still am looking for the concrete proof besides personal experience. I am calm in all types of situations and don't let my imagination get the better of me. In any case I know I would be your best bet as a fellow investigator!

Investigator Comments:

Concrete proof of the paranormal is still a long ways out. Being calm in all situations and thinking through things is essential when investigating the paranormal. This level-headed approach backed by a good knowledge of the field will help get the proof that is needed to move the field forward. Keep up the great work!

I Wanna Be Your Bitch

Thursday, March 26, 2009 6:00 PM
From: Sammy, Waukesha, WI

I've been looking around for some time now for a serious investigation group to join. I LOVE the paranormal. I love everything about it! I am in it for the LONG HALL and this is what I want to do for a living.

I'm not a bitch or anything, but I love the paranormal sooooo much that I am willing to allw you to use me as your bitch. Do with me what you will! I'm all yours, just let me join your group and come with you on investigations.

Call me and we can talk more about it.

thanks

Investigator Comments:

Hmmmmm....Well, although we LOVE your enthusiasm and eagerness to help us with anything we need, we really don't need a bitch nor would we want a bitch. We truly need someone who is able to research, investigate, and comprehend the true science of the paranormal. If that's you, then that's GREAT! Let's talk! (Oh, yeah...and one more thing. Get me a beer, bitch!!)

Chapter Five

The "Boo" Heard 'Round the World

This chapter focuses on emails we've received from people all over the world.

Gravesite of an unknown woman.

Unsolved Murders Psychic?

Thursday, February 15, 2007 1:00 PM
From: Tyra, Ft. Wayne, IN

have you seen or can you see spirits from unsolved murders and help solve them? I know of one unsolved murder in Janesville that I can't seem to forget. Please respond by e-mail only. thank you.

Investigator Comments:

We are about as psychic as rocks. We actually have very few experiences, so we don't think we will be able to detect spirits from unsolved murders. If we come across a good psychic who specializes in unsolved murders, we will be sure to get in touch. It is actually surprising how many police departments use information from psychics when trying to solve murders.

Haunted House Frightens Me!

Thursday, February 6, 2003 11:51 AM
From: Heidi, Newland, NC

There is a house near where I live that has some very bad stories connected to it. Everyone I take past it gets an uncomfortabel feeling about it. I don't like to look at it, and drive by as fast as I can. I am actually afraid of the house. I think it may be of some interest to you. I don't know much about it, but there are many people who have lived in this area who are familiar with it.

Investigator Comments:

Once again, someone asked us about a house that we have no idea where it is or what has happened there. This one is even better because they don't seem to know much about it either. More information would be beneficial. We are curious as to why the house makes them afraid. Is it the way it looks? The stories associated with it? Do they feel creeped out by any other houses? Maybe the next time we are in Newland, North Carolina, we will try to locate it and drive by to see what happens.

Chichen Itza

Thursday, February 24, 2005 5:22 PM
From: David, York, PA

has your group ever investigated Chichen Itza in the Yucutan in Mexico? I just got back from a trip to there and it was really awesome! You can just feel the ancient energy go through you when you are at Chichen Itza! I was the most amazing and overpowering experience that I have ever had. All the history and all the things that happened there would no doubt mean that it is haunted by something from the past. Just standing there you can feel the presence of all those who lived and died there. I'm pretty sure I felt what the Mayans felt when they were there. The power of the universe seemed to be directed right at me when I stood on top of the Pyramid Kukulcan Temple. It was a long hot climb to the top of the this ancient pyramid but once you are at the top you realize how worth the climb it was! The view is simply breath taking. There is a total feeling of energy and awesomeness that I have never experienced before! After soaking up the universal energy from the top of the pyramid I climbed back down since I was eager to explore more of this powerful ancient site. I made my way to the Great Ball court where they would have these games that ended in death for the winning team. The person showing us the site said those games would go on for weeks sometimes. I guess no one really wanted to win cause the tour guide told us that the winning team would usually be sacrificed to the Mayan gods. I guess I wouldn't be to eager to win a game if my reward was to be sacarficed. But I guess it was considered an honor for them. Anyway, this ball court ewas amazing. You could whisper at one end and someone could hear what you were saying on the other end of the stadium. I saw this image carved into the stone in the stadium. It was one of the players who had been decapitated. I assumed he must have been on the winning team! Hahahaha. Wow, right? There were all kinds of really cool carvings in the rocks. At one point when everyone was being quite I could clearly hear the past. I heard the voices on the ancient players yelling and screaming. I think this was truly an amazing paranormal experience! I was hoping to maybe see one of the ancient Mayans walk right in front of me but that didn't happen. Maybe next time. Then I walked over to one of the big sink holes that they call cenote. It was filled with water so it looked like a pond in the bottom of a hole. The big one that was really amazing was the Sagrado Cenote (sink hole). This is where the Mayans would sacrifice people. I wonder if any scuba divers have gone down there and seen humain remains. I would love to do that. At one point I heard a scream and thought I saw something fall off the other side and fall into the water. It was really weird cause I didn't hear or see and splash like if someone really did fall into the water. I think I may have gone back in time and saw a real human sacrifice. That is the only thing that would make sense to me. I am very psychic and have experiences all the time so it wouldn't surprise me if I did see something beyond this world when I was at this ancient historic location. Maybe your group could go down and investigate this place sometime. If you do I would love to help you out and I could tell you where all the good spots are.

Investigator Comments:

We have never been there, but we hear it is going to be the place to be when the end comes. Take Mayan word for it, it's gonna be a BLAST!

Ghost Gab Paranormal Talk Show

Saturday, October 1, 2005, 5:26 AM
From: Stuart, Worthing, West Sussex, England

Hi there! I have just listened to your first episode about Paranormal Groups and Private Invesigations. Being a Co-founder of an organisation which has been established for some 10 years it was refreshing to hear that there are others who have similar morals/ethics/techniques as ourselves. I agree that there are too many 'time wasters' out there. Unfortunately in this country we have to thank 'Most Haunted' (bad paranormal entertainment programme) for the upsurge of these type groups. We are lucky that we have a very experienced group of individuals and everyone appears to pull together (especially helpful when we get a 'nasty' spirit through.

We always say to private investigation locations that if they want to make a contribution to the cost involved in travelling to the location then they are more than welcome too but they are always told they don't have to. Most of the time they feed us while we are there (not a bad when you like food like I do.

I look forward to listening to your further programmes and wish you well in your endeavours. If by chance you are ever over this side of the water then do feel free to drop me a line, we always welcome a chat with fellow investigators.

Regards

Stuart

Co-Founder/Research Manager

C.O.T.C Paranormal Investigations

Investigator Comments:

We thank you for your kind email! Glad you enjoyed *Ghost Gab*. We had lots of fun doing the show and thought it was a good way to get information out. It's great to hear from a fellow experienced and serious investigator. If we make it across the big pond, we will be sure to get in touch with you. Good luck and keep up the great work!

Colombia Ghost Chasers

Friday, May 29, 2009, 2:51 PM
From: Carlos, Medellin, Colombia

Cordial and respectful greeting

My name is Carlos and I am founder of the Group of psychic Investigation and of phenomenons paranormales GRIS ENIGMA of Medellin, Colombia.

I have visited your web and I find that you are very organized and that your work is serious and of quality. I want to know that possibilities are that our Group and your Group share information and, because not, some day, to make a combined investigation.

My team is conformed by a group of professionals in different areas: (Psychology, Electronic, Theology, Sociology, graphic Design and Systems) guided to the investigation by the scientific method of phenomenons paranormales and of extrasensorial perception with base in Medellin, Colombia.

Our Investigators in Medellin, are the following ones:

Marina, Educational, Humanist and clinical psychologist, Investigator of Field

Marcos, National Boss of Security, Technician in electronic, Expert in Technical of Judicial Investigation, in charge of the security in the land

Iván, National Boss of Rites and Protocols, Investigator of Field, Advisory of protocols

Carlos, National Coordinator of Investigators, Investigator of Field, Sensitive.

Edith, Medical Obstetrician
Vilma, Psychologist
Olga, Psychologist
Astrid, Theologian, Humanist, Physical Medium
Olver, Technician in electronic, psychic Medium
Huber, Graduate in Humanities, Investigator of Field
Carolina, Sensitive, Investigator of Field
Edwin, Educational , analyst of information
Leomán, Analyst of information, Advisory technological
Víctor, Analyst of information, Advisory technological
Claudia, Investigator of Field
Carolina, Investigator of Field
Claudia, Investigator of Field

Our group is not sponsored by any company and when we make investigations we make it with our own resources. Neither we have good mensuration teams but if we have a responsible, serious and dedicated human team.

I hope it enters to our it paginates and knows us and we can establish a friendly relationship and of mutual collaboration.

Thank you for their valuable time

Investigator Comments:

Now, this team seems to have it together! There is a nice mix of individuals from different fields. Having differing perspectives from many people in various specialized areas is good since we are not sure what we are dealing with. It is actually rare to find a group that is willing to go on investigations together. It is even rarer to find a group that is willing to share information. We have noticed a real lack of people sharing their data, information, and techniques. This is crazy. Especially when a vast majority of groups proclaim they are science based and follow the scientific method. A major component of the scientific method is to publish data and results and allow others to comment on and replicate their work.

Why is there such a turf war in the paranormal community? One of the main reasons is that people are in it for the wrong reasons. They want to be famous. They either have no data or they are holding onto it for the TV show they may never get. The other reason may be because they don't want anyone to critique their work and information. They want their data to support their belief that there is life after death and any comment to the contrary will be rejected, sometimes viciously.

It is refreshing to have other groups reach out and want to share their information and collaborate. This is exactly what the field needs to move forward.

You've Lost That Stonehenge Feeling

Friday, May 11, 2007, 10:21 PM
From: Steve, Edgerton, WI

I was wondering if anyone has ever told about ay paranormal experiences from Stonehenge? I know there have been reports of crop circles and UFOs and weird demon animals spoted around that area but what about ghosts?

I was there visiting with my friends one day and it was getting kinda late. The sun was starting to go down and I told everyone that I think we should get goin. I was pretty uncomfortable the entire time we was there. It really felt like someone was watching me. You know...that creep feelin you get when you know something isn't right and you think something from anoher diemsion is watching you?

I really wanted to go but the people I was with just didn't want to go. Then I thought I saw something. It looked like this dark figure was darting around the big rocks. I thought what the heck, right. Maybe it was just the light playin some tricks on me eyes because it was getting dark out. I kept watching and this dark figure would go in and out between the rocks. I was getting pretty freaked out so I asked one of the people I was with uis they had seen it. They said no and thought I was acting a little off. Now, I know we were both looking in the exact sane spot when I saw the dark figure run from one rock to another. I was like holy shit! You didn't just see that? And they said no. After that I hurried back to the car and waitd for the rest of them to get back and then we left. I was really scared and I don't know if I would ever go back to thet place again.

Have you heard of anything like that happenin there?

Investigator Comments:

How about we forward this to the COTC group from England?

Canadian Premonition

Thursday, July 17, 2008, 7:44 PM
From: Dougie, Toronto, Canada

Hello. I wanted to tell you about something interesting that happened to me the other day. I know your group is in the US and I am in Canada but this is a pretty interesting story.

I had these dreams the last few nights about my daughter wondering off and then ending up drowned in a swimming pool. I would wake up each night and be really upset about this dream.

Now it gets pretty weird cause one morning I woke up and turned the TV on and was watching the news. And there was this story about this political person from the US that had fallen in her swimming pool and drowned! I thought that was pretty weird cause I had been havin those dreams about my daughter drowning in a swimming pool.

Now the person on the news was not related to me in anyway but I was wondering if maybe I had a premonition with those dreams.

Please let me know what you might think about this.

Thank you kindly.

Investigator Comments:

This is most likely coincidence. Many people have dreams that involve their children drowning. This is a common fear among parents, therefore, it is not surprising that parents would have this bad dream fairly often. There are 1.2 million people world wide who die each year from drowning. That translates to more than 2 people per minute. So, having a dream about a child drowning, then seeing a story on TV about a drowning, could very easily happen.

Chapter Six

WTF?

This chapter focuses on emails we received from people who were so unique, we didn't know what to do with them. These emails were strange, funny, demented, crazy, goofy, and some lacked information in such a way, they just made us say, "What?" After you read a few, we're sure you'll understand!

Bear Spirit

Friday, January 1, 2010 7:27 AM
From: Susan, Stoughton, WI

> I smudged my home with sage and dragon's blood during the blue moon on the new year and as I did so in one room saw the shape of a bear lumbering away out of a room and disappear. I have searched for the significance of this spirit (a bear) as my home is not an older home nor is it built (at least I don't think it's built) on the site of any sacred ground.
>
> Your thoughts?

Investigator Comments:

Hmmmm....first of all, where did you get dragon's blood? I thought that wasn't in season till the spring? Sounds like a great way to bring in the New Year! Not sure what the bear means. We would suggest looking into animal spirits and spirit guides and see if that makes any sense. Or at least makes more sense than this e-mail.

Slightly annoyed orange-eyed entity.

Orange-Eyed Entity

Tuesday, August 4, 2009 7:28 PM
From: JoAnne, Petersburg, WI

Hi- I don't mean to bother you (or the orange eyed entity in my home) but lately, there has been a flurry of activity, my son has seen a man in his fifies with orange eyes in the basement and a ton of other stuff. My sister was trying to take a picture of her daughter in a room bathed with light and the shot came out comepletely black with a red figure in the corner. I tried to replicate the shot using her camera and my camera- to no avail. I was wondering, what advice you may have, or if you investigate these things? there have been numerous instances where everyone in the house heard voices, seen shadows, etc. what ever it is seems to prefer those that are senstive to it.

Please contact me asap- I would greatly appreciate it, we're onto something here, and I don't know what to do. I will try and upload that picture tomorrow. my sis doesn't have a pc or the cord to upload it to mine. thank so very much in advance!

Investigator Comments:

You didn't bother us but we can't speak for the orange-eyed entity. We do investigate these things. In order to get a better feel for what is going on, we ask people to answer a variety of different questions. After they return the questions, we review them, schedule a pre-investigation, do a full investigation if needed, review the data, write a report, and then reveal our findings to the client. We also discuss various ways they can deal with the situation. It isn't surprising that whatever this thing is prefers those who are sensitive to it. It seems as if different people have different levels of sensitivity. And obviously those who are more sensitive will have more experiences. We find it more fascinating when people who are not sensitive and haven't had prior experiences have an experience. As far as advice...we always tell people to keep a journal noting the who, what, when and where each time something happens. This really helps get a feel for the situation. We also tell people to not be scared. Take control! It is their house. This empowerment will make people feel better and help alleviate any fear they may have.

Ghostly Activity

Friday, July 4, 2008 8:40 AM
From: Jeffrey, West Allis, WI

I have ghostly activity and it's pretty freaky

there's A Building In WV Which Is Haunted it's Haunted Because I Talked To The Manager And He Said A few Years Ago A Matenience Personal Walked Up To The Third Floor And saw A Apparetion Standing there And He Ran Back To His Office then He Heard Furniture Being Moved And Thought Well Who Would Be Having A Meeting At This Time Of Night So He Went Upstairs And Nobody Was There.

Investigator Comments:

Well, obviously this place must be haunted.

Illiterate Ghosts

Tuesday, December 4, 2007 8:51 PM
From: Lori, West Allis, WI

Greetings!

I was on the net looking for info on hauntings and found your email address. I have lived in my home since 1998 here in West Allis and am convinced that I have my share of spooks. I have never seen anything but have heard lots of noises that cause me to check the house over for intruders. It seems to happen the most during the day when I am there alone. I have heard some one come in the house and go into the basement only to find nobody their. My TV has also gone on by itself. It is nothing that crepes me out but I have had other people get a little freeked out by their experiences. The latest one was this mourning which sounded like the toilet lid being droped and something being droped on the floor with foot steps and ofcourse, nobody their.

Thanks

Investigator Comments:

Just because you never see a ghost, doesn't mean it isn't haunted. Actually, seeing a ghost is pretty rare. Hearing, smelling, and sensing something is much more common. Object movement is also common in hauntings.

Rockford Ghosts

Tuesday, October 23, 2007 3:47 PM
From: Daisy, Rockford, IL

I saw an article about you in Rockford Register Star online. I grew up in the Rockford area. I remember a story that was in the papers back in, 1981 I think? About a family on the east side that thought they had a ghost. The mother of the family would get out of the shower and find little bite or scratch marks on her body, unexplained, and there was something about an old living room chair left over in the basement by the previous owners. Did anyone in your group ever hear about this and if so, had there ever been any followup?

Happy Halloween!

Investigator Comments:

The reason this email was placed in this chapter is because there are *soooo* many times we get asked very specific questions about an area, location, or event and are given little or no information except for a second-person account of an incident. This annoys the HELL out of us!! Are we just expected to know everything about all haunted locations? Every story ever told in an area? We get these all the time and all we can really say is, "Arrrgghhh!"

Premonitions

Thursday, October 18, 2007 10:53 AM
From: Bob, Never Neverland

Do you believe in people having preminations in their sleep. So electrafying it is like being pulled down under your bed but after you get away there is nothing there. I was in a car accident in 1999 and this happened after the accident. In the accident my seat belt was ripped off me and I was thrown into the back seat on the floor on my head. And the first 4 months after this accident wierd things happened. Can you explain?

Investigator Comments:

First of all, I need to express an urgency of what I'm about to say next. GO SEE A DOCTOR!! You may have head trauma.

Dark Presence in Oak Creek

Saturday, October 6, 2007 12:04 PM
From: Jimmy, Oak Creek, WI

I stayed at an apartment complex for less than a year in Oak Creek, WI. The apartment had been vacant for quite some time, and there was a dark presence in the apartment that would only visit in the middle of the night - maybe about 2 or 3am. I didn't think anything of it when I signed the lease, but it figures. The airplanes always came in right over the apartment. I can't remember the rest of the address now.

Investigator Comments:

Again, "Aaaarrggghhhh!!!" Did you hit your head, too?

Paranoramal Activity Possibly?

Sunday, July 15, 2007 8:56 PM
From: Amy, Wisconsin Dells, WI

I have been recently hooked on the t.v. show on the Discovery Channel called A Haunting. After watching it was hooked on it and have seen different types of hauntings etc., as of recently my boyfriend and I have been experencing various abnormal activity. I tried doing some research about it and believe that It may possibly be a form of a poltergeist. I have been experiencing things such as the door slamming shut out of nowhere, while driving in my boyfriends car the doors will unlock and all of his windows will roll down as well as the sun roof opening up, and also we both have a weird feeling of being watched.

Do you think that you may be able to help me better understand what is going on and if i may be going crazy. Thanks

Investigator Comments:

A brief review of the different types of ghosts and hauntings would be appropriate. The first is known as a residual haunting or what some people call, "place memory." It is a moment in time that is somehow recorded in the environment. The event recorded is highly emotional in nature, either good or bad. Then under the right conditions and with the right person, the event replays itself. It is like a video loop playing over and over. There is no interaction between the living and the phenomenon. The second is the true "dead-guy" apparitions. This is the part of the human consciousness that survives bodily death. It displays intelligence and interacts with the people witnessing it. The third is poltergeist activity or what is termed, Recurrent Spontaneous Psychokinesis, "RSPK." It has nothing to do with a ghost or dead guy. It involves a living person known as the agent. This person is under some sort of stress and is releasing the stress subconsciously by affecting things in the environment. The object affected in the environment is symbolic to the things causing the stress. It is impossible to determine what is going on based on the information provided. It could be one thing or a combination of things. In order to appropriately address a situation, it is paramount to know what type of activity we might be dealing with.

Mobile Home Ghosts

Tuesday, July 25, 2006 8:03 AM
From: Babette, Little Chute, WI

my boyfriends sister is experiencing some paranormal activities in the mobile home she lives in. Her husband was asleep and he said that someone was pulling on his legs. He was the only one there. She was home by herself and there was a knock at the door. there was no one there. tv will shut off by itself. doors will open and close and she could hear a woman speak spanish in the other room when no one else is home.

Investigator Comments:

We love to get reports of paranormal activity. But there isn't much we can do if the person who is having the experience isn't the one who contacts us. At least give us their e-mail address or phone number.

Amazing Discovery!

Saturday, March 25, 2006 3:05 PM
From: Granville, Zion, IL

Some may considr this paranormal but I would not, this discovery can be taught to most anyone but I think it ill help to understand some paranormal things and give a lot of answers. I need scientist journalist media and help launching this to the world.

Hello, I have been trying for a very long time now to get someone to take me serious about a very big discovery that I have which will help in Science and Archeology as well as geology and world history. There just seems to be no end to even more new information all the time from this discovery. It seems to be able to give answers to many world wonders. I can do satellite imaging or photo imaging better than anyone around the world using the knowledge from my discovery better than anyone can even better than anything than any military ever could. But there is much more to this than just imaging.

I have found that this system of things we call earth and all things that exist in and around it has been recording images since the beginning of time and I found how to get these images. These images I am talking about are of people/animals and plants objects and even events from the worlds past , so no doubt that these things are being recorded today but at this time I am not sure how to get very recent images perhaps there some time has to pass before they become developed? I am sure in time some scientist could figure out much more than I have found out so far. I am sure this is the biggest news the world could ever hear to this date.

Because of the way this works I can show how to get images from Stone Henge or the Pyramids of people doing what they were doing and events which will tell many things we do not know or help correct things we think we know. At this time I know quite a lot about many things that I will not bother to mention because one must know how this works and that it really does work before you will believe me.

I MUST SHOW HOW THIS WORKS IN PERSON - it is too hard to convince anyone of such wonders and seeing is believing. I can get images of objects under the ground and I can see a single coin in the desert and many coins where there are treasures. I have located many things that I will be traveling to collect very soon. I purchased a large motor home so that I can travel the USA. I am very close to selling my home and going on the road. I figure I need to collect a few treasures I have found and it should work out just about right to get someone to do a documentary about my find after I have found a few treasures.

I would love to show NASA how this works because they are missing out on a lot of information that they need to know. Again- Because of the way this works I can show how the same process will work to tell if there ever was life on mars or other planets. If there ever was life on another planet I can show what that life looked like and images of objects etc. I can show how they can know in just one day or no more than a week if there ever was life on mars and more.

While this all sounds to much to be true, you have not heard nothing yet. Like I said there just seems to be no end to even more information or discoveries and the whole world needs to be involved in this.

NASA wants me to submit a non solicited proposal form which will not work for me in the way I need to get the information to them or present it to them. With someones help I may get to show them what I have discovered.

I am not a scientist but many years of work went into my research that has led to this discovery. You will not be disappointed if you visit with me or have someone visit with me before I go on the road and see that there is much more to my discovery than I have mentioned. Perhaps you could forward this to someone who could look into this? I do have a couple of well known publisher/journalist wanting to do a story on this but I need someone who can travel a little with me to document a few things first. This would be the biggest on going story that the history channel or discovery channel could ever get.

I can show how this will work under water but it is much harder to do.

Thanks.

Granville

Investigator Comments:

WOW!

Amazing Discovery...Part Deux!

Monday, February 22, 2010 4:42 PM
From: Granville. Zion, IL

After emailing this author to ask if they would give us permission to print their story in my book, they sent the following reply...

Hi, I am so excited that you would want to put this in a book and without even looking at what I had written I can go over the discovery again if it will help or if it could be written better than I can write.

I have been doing research for quite a lot of years now into something I discovered and I am trying to improve my research methods but I really need the help of scientist and Colleges everywhere. I also beg NASA to get with me and let me show them how to find life on other planets. I will give you permission to publish or print what I am writing in this letter but the rights to my discovery and claims remain to be my property. You do not need to pay me for writing that which is written in this letter.

Many years ago I discovered that this system of things we call Earth has a way of recording images of People objects and events that are now images from the worlds past and I can teach people how to get these images but! I will only do it in person because it is just to hard to teach unless it is in person. BUT! in person it is not that hard to learn and do. I could have you seeing images in just a matter of minutes and the longer you do it the better you can get. People are always seeing images that they think are the Madonna or Christ, or the Virgin Mary. Chances are that these images are not who they think they are. I know that these images are everywhere around the world and I can go anywhere around the world and get these images. It can be done on water but it is much harder. There are images on the ocean floor but I don't know the reason they are there and as a matter of fact I don't know why there are images anywhere. I'm sure God has the answers. I can use Satellites to get images of people objects and events , also can use photography to do the same thing. I can teach you so well that you can learn to see images. NOW if any of you don't believe me it is easy to find out because I will teach this to the right people such as archaeologist, Scientist, { Sientist want to disprove this type of thing and I welcome them to disprove it BUT! they must eventually admit that it works when I prove it over and over the same results. Also since I can find objects lost for years or under ground that means I can find treasures and It was my intention to go collect some of these treasures but my divorce set me back where it will be hard for me to afford the things I needed to do it the way I wanted. BUT! it would not take that much money to do it . I was going to get a $33.000 full body ultra light helicopter that would get me to remote places to do an aerial of the area I wanted to search. You see I have even found single coin images in some desolate places and sometimes a treasure trove which I book marked and even got a 250 Gig storage device to hold my images but one day I had a computer crash and never was able to recover the images and or get any from the encripted hard drive. } LOST but! that does not mean I have no images , I can get images all day long every day but it wqas yeaqrs of my finest work lost. I am thinking about getting me a smaller camper and go to some key locations and start looking for some treasures and when I get one I will have the funding for the others.

With my imaging I can go to places like Stonehenge and show them how to learn more about what stonehenge was about. Also The Nasca lines in Peru, I can show them much more than they know about that area. Same with Pyramids and wonders of the world.

Then there is the illusive search for Noah's Ark some say it is in the mountains in Turkey and I try and image that area and get nothing BUT! I found something that may have been it ???? In New Mexico and I also found a lot of other interesting things there. I don't think there was an ocean in New Mexico around Cabazon peak but! I found images of ships with a man standing on deck that was looking off over the horizon as if he is looking out over the waters of the ocean. He was wearing a hat or helment that looked to be like a 13 century spanyard . Now I doubt there was an ocean there at that time but could I be wrong in dateing the image? There is images of other ships in the area. Have you ever saw images in clouds that looked like people or animals? you are just getting a small glimpse into my discovery. I suggest to you if you see a good image in a cloud and it starts to disipate or go away keep watching because if you happen to be there for the first image then there may be several more of the exact same image. It does happen and it does work if you happen to be there when it is first formed.

Energy in power lines has images also I have one to prove it also. I used to have quite a lot of images but lost many. But I can get them again in time. All my years of work lost. Have you ever saw an image on a rock or something that looked like an image? It is from the same source. [TO the person writing the book} If you could believe enough to come take a look for once in your life see something that really works with no hoax of any kind.

Perhaps somehow the images I can get are where the images of the paranormal come from. I also Think I have saw images of something that died but it would be something that looks like a lilly with a string running through it and it is going up and up into the sky with a string going through many lilly's and some will tilt one way or the other and blow around like a tail of a kite. I have saw that which I consider to be the most incredidable art you could ever see. I sure wish I was an artist and could paint what I can see and most anyone can see what I see if they will only start out with an open mind and do as I say and work at it.

I don't walk around with blinders on and I notice many things most people don't pay any attention to. There is one thing I seem to have always known, I won't bother trying to explain it here you will find it too hard to believe. BUT! All over the world there is one image I keep seeing and it is a MAN that has equipment much like a surveyor and draftsman. It is as tho this was the creator or helper????? I call him my little buddy. I think I have saw quite a lot into the past with this discovery. I also think or am pretty sure I have saw a aircraft that can only be ancient and have saw it in several places and have one solid image of it.

How about life on other planets? Because of the way this works I can show how to tell if there was life on other planets with the use of NASA's images. One of my most perfect images was lost with the computer crash. I wish I knew exactly which image I got it from? of NASA's . It was sdo perfect . A picture of life from another planet BUT! I can find othere.

I offered James Randi a challenge to disprove my claims but he would not let me retain the rights to my discovery and I would have even shared the rights just so I could show the world but he refused to do it.

With people making claims or guessing about things like Nasca Lines or Stonehenge or other wonders it sure would be nice to see something that actually is for real and really works for a change. I kringe when I see things on discovery or history channel when I know something they don't know.

I sure wish I could show the world. Take my word for it I CAN ROCK THE WORLD!!!

Yes you can publish this information and I still retain the right to use my own words or discovery that you are writing about. I am very glad for your intrest. I CAN ROCK THE WORLD! when no one else can prove their claims I can show you all the proof the world could need and classrooms would all be teaching my works.

Thanks so very much dear.

Granville

Investigator Comments:

WOW! WOW!

Bloopie The Dragon

Sunday, February 12, 2006 3:13 PM
From: Alisha, Superior, WI

I have seen lights simlar to this in my bedroom. they were not that spread out but were weaving between the fan blades and moving toward the closet door and back to the fan blades. I asked who it was there and I was given the answer Bloopie. Bloopie is a dragon that a friend of mine talked about and apparently came in with that person. I aske what they wanted and was told my grandson. I asked if they were of God was told no I told them they would have to leave and I have not seen them since.

Investigator Comments:

Is Bloopie Puff's little brother? Did Bloopie get into Puff's stash? Have you ever seen Bloopie the magical dragon? Have you ever seen Bloopie the magical dragon...on weed?

Not Ghosts

Sunday, February 12, 2006 1:54 PM
From: Barbara, Onalaska, WI

I have been listening to the Sassy house tapes They are speaking in an ancient language. I didn't understand the exact words but they were discussing the group and equipment and unsure of your intent. They were spirits. NOT GHOSTS The second recording is the same language. One is saying "they are leaving"

Investigator Comments:

The Sassy House investigation is one of our best cases! The owner first called because she was upset about an alien who came through the portal in her closet and illegally took the spirit of her dog and the dog died. She spent $700 for an autopsy and various tests. No reason for the dog dying could be found.

When we first talked to the owner, we weren't sure how much we could help her since we didn't deal with aliens. We were wondering why an illegal spirit was taking a dog soul. Do you need a permit from the DNR to make it legal? Anyway…we weren't going take the case, then the owner told us about the other paranormal activity that was going on. This included strange odors, object movement, footsteps, and her brother being pulled out of bed by his feet. Now this seemed more like what we were used to dealing with on a haunting case. We decided to visit the owner for a pre-investigation.

When we first arrived, the owner took us to the backyard where she showed us her crop circle. Her inverted crop circle. She had planted corn in a circle and created an inverted crop circle. Interesting. We then heard about the ghosts of two slave children that were in the garage.

Upon going inside, the owner shared an interesting story. She said she had fallen asleep one day around noon and woke up around 3PM. When she looked out the window she saw a bright ball of light outside! She asked us what we thought it was and we both could only think of one thing, THE SUN! Next we took a tour of the house and the owner explained where and what happened in various locations throughout the house. We video recorded the entire time. At one point, we went upstairs, looked around, and then went back downstairs. The owner said she forgot to tell us something about the second floor so we all went back up to the second-floor bedroom. As we entered the bedroom, we noticed the radio next to the bed was on. We didn't think it was on before so we reviewed the video and it had not been on when we were upstairs in the room five minutes earlier. As we discussed the situation, the radio got louder on its own! This event caused us to take the case and conduct a full investigation. And we are glad we did!

After the investigation, we were reviewing the audio recordings and discovered two very interesting EVPs! The first sounded like three different creepy voices talking and moaning. The second EVP was shocking! It seemed as if it was interacting with the conversation between two investigators. Simply amazing! We were excited to share our findings with the owner.

We traveled back to her house to reveal our findings. While playing the EVPs for her we all clearly heard five to six heavy footsteps run across the second floor. Not only did we hear them, but we felt the vibrations from each step. We ran upstairs and confirmed no one was up there. We did our best to debunk what we had just experienced, but be could find no natural explanation. We went back downstairs and the owner said, "I'm so glad you heard that! That is exactly what I have been experiencing. Now I know I'm not crazy!"

Guardian Angels and Spirit Guides

Sunday, February 12, 2006 8:41 AM
From: Patricia, Washington Island, WI

I have my house filled with Guardian Angles and Spirit Guides. They speak to me all the time thru thought transfer. My computer printer cartridge with move when the printer is shut off. My house with crack in a certain rhythm. They asked me to have you to come and have a chat. We are a Christian household.

I do not communican with ghosts. They do not stay by me. I will keep written records for a month and you can come and chat with them and see if they tell you the same thing. I have smells and when a friend was dying of cancer they would sit on my bed and pat my leg until I would fall asleep.

Investigator Comments:

The appropriate term in parapsychology for thought transfer is, "telepathy." "My house with crack..." Ummm, no comment. Fortunately we are not psychic or sensitive and therefore don't talk with spirits, so we could pass on this one.

Odors?

Tuesday, June 10, 2003 5:56 PM
From: Mary, Madison, WI

Hsve seen Mist. Heard noises. Seen ghost from different decades. Light orbs. Screaming and talking. Oders.

Investigator Comments:

And??? Orbs and screaming and odors...
Oh my! WTF???

Chapter Seven

We Came, We Saw, We Wrote a Report!

This chapter features the original inquiries we received requesting an investigation accompanied by the completed investigation report.

The Carver House Haunting

From: Home owners (who requested to remain anonymous)

Original Investigation Request was received on: Tuesday, August 12, 2008 7:28 PM

I believe the spirit of my husband's deceased wife is haunting us, removing objects from our house and most of the time returning them but some things have never been returned. This has been going on ever since my husband and I got married on 11-01-2003 and I can't handle it much longer. It's obvious she doesn't want me in the house as all of the things that have been removed belonged to me and NONE from my husband. Pleae let me know how soon you can do an investigation. Thank you

Shortly after receiving this email, Jennifer Lauer, Founder & Executive Director of the SWPRG, sent an email along with a set of questions required for everyone seeking an investigation. The questions must be fill-out and returned to SWPRG. The home owners filled out the questions and mailed them back to us.

A Pre-Investigation was completed on: Thursday, October 16, 2008, 6PM

A pre-investigation of the location is necessary, takes anywhere from one to two hours, and only requires two investigators. At this stage of the process the investigators will:

1. Take a tour of the location and videotape the entire location.
2. Videotape the witnesses as they explain where and what has been happening in the location.
3. Take baseline readings – environmental readings taken during this stage will allow investigators to understand and document the full range of natural and man-made power sources and other activity coming from the property.
4. Try to find natural explanations for paranormal reports.
5. Evaluate pre-investigation data to determine if full-investigation is warranted.

Additional Information was received from home owner on: Sunday, November 16, 2008 6:11 AM

Good Morning Jennifer,

I don't know why I didn't think of this last night but I guess you would call this an unusual happening.

Around the end of Sept.I could hear noises when we were in the computer room early in the morning. At first we thought there were squirrels running around on the roof because they do that a lot. There's a black walnut tree in the back yard and they would collect the black walnuts that would drop and play with them on the roof, we would see opened and crushed walnuts on the steps and sidewalk. Well, the noises got louder and we thought they were too loud, too close, and no longer thought they were squirrels. At one point my husband was sure he heard two animals fighting - he heard a growl-like noise. That's when he decided to call an exterminator, he did that on October 9.

The exterminator came on Oct. 9, and found a hole dug outside just out from our kitchen window. He put out 3 traps in that area and on Oct. 11 he came and removed 1 opossum. On Oct. 12 he came and removed 1 raccoon. On Oct. 17 he removed another raccoon. On Oct. 22 he removed he removed another opossum and finally on Oct. 24 removed another raccoon. He waited a couple of days and decided he got all the animals and he closed up the hole with concrete on Oct. 27, 2008.

We talked about this today and my husband said he thinks the animals could have gotten as far as in the basement ceiling over the main basement room. He said that when he was cleaning down there he could detect an animal smell but never could find evidence that any of the animals had actually been in the basement. He claims the smell is gone now. We have not heard any more noises in the computer room either, so I guess the animals are all gone now that the hole they dug is closed with concrete.

I don't think we have had any other unusual events, but I certainly will let you know if we do. I expect it will be quiet around here after your visit, like it was the last time you were here, when it was quiet for several days to a week.

Additional Information was received from home owner on: Monday, August 31, 2009 2:17 PM

Hi Jennifer,

I just called your office but ran out of "talking time" on your answering machine. I want to finish up my call by saying thank you for listening.

When I listened to my voice, it was quite shaky. I'm sorry for that but I have not been feeling well, some days are worse than others, but stomach is quite queasy and nauseous most days - except the days that I am away from this house. There are a lot of days when I can hardly eat enough to keep my blood sugar from dropping, and that's scary.

I certainly hope you are feeling better and you will be able to set up a reveal date soon. Like I said on the phone, the results that you will explain to us will determine whether or not I can continue to live in this house. Whoever has been haunting us for the last 6 years, still leaves little signs that she is still here, and I believe that she, (he, or it) seems to be here all the time. When we went to N. Michigan in July we decided not to leave any lights on in the house. When we returned, the kitchen light was on. Almost every time we go out for the evening, our bedroom light will be on when we get home.

The last real scary event was when we returned from N. Wisconsin in mid-July. I had purchased a cobalt blue electric lamp the size of a hurricane lamp. My 2 sister-in-laws were with me and talked me into buying a white glass lamp shade to go on it. When I got ready to put the lamp on a cabinet in the living room, the lamp shade all of a sudden was in about 8 or 9 pieces on the floor and I was still holding the lamp UPRIGHT!!! That really shook me up.

I hope to see you and Cindy real soon, or whoever you bring with you.

Please let me hear from you!

The official report shown below was revealed to the home owners on: Sunday, October 11, 2009 3PM

The Carver House Investigations

November 15, 2008 & January 24, 2009
Report prepared by Jennifer Lauer

Introduction & Background

The family contacted the SWPRG because of a variety of unexplained items they have noticed missing since April 2003. These items included:

- A large suitcase on wheels
- Coffee pot still in its original box
- A plastic bag containing 2 small blue bathroom rugs
- A storage box containing knitting needles, crochet needles, and other accessories
- Curtain rod from the dining room
- Audio tapes
- A stewing pot
- Knickknacks

Some of these items have been found either in the same location they have been missing from or in another location where they should not be. Other unexplainable events have included:

- A coffee pot that turns on and begins brewing 1 hour prior to the scheduled time on 3 separate occasions
- The dryer door opened by itself after the dryer shut off
- Footsteps have been heard on the kitchen floor

These events have been experienced in each of the following rooms in the house:

- Basement
- Master bedroom closet
- Toy room including closet
- Computer room closet
- Kitchen
- Dining room
- Living room

No one from outside of the household has experienced anything out of the ordinary and all of the items that have gone missing have been the property of the female homeowner. The objects have never been witnessed moving or appearing/disappearing. They have only been noticed after the fact. The homeowners have speculated that these occurrences could possibly be caused by the male homeowner's deceased first wife who had previously resided in the home.

The female homeowner has stated that the more events that happen, the more frustrated and tense she becomes. She has experienced several occasions of stomach distress, nausea, and/or heartburn; and she attributes the stress to the disturbances in the home. She had a CAT scan in November of 2007 which revealed no problems.

Materials & Methods:

A pre-investigation was conducted on October 16th, 2008, and two full investigations were done on both November 15th, 2008, and January 24th, 2009.

Equipment used:

- Non-contact IR thermal probe scanner
- Tri-field natural EMF meter
- Tri-field meter
- Temperature gauge
- EMF gauss meter
- Hall Effect Gauss meter from Integrity Design and Research Corporation. (A bare probe was used with the gauss meter. The bandwidth of the bare probe is 68Hz at 3dB.)
- Air ion Counter. (Positive and negative ion counts are displayed as ions/cm3.)
- Direct Environmental Acquisition Data logging system

(DEAD)
- A Psyleron Quantum Based Random Number Generator (QRNG)

Investigation Team:

Jennifer Lauer
Judy Dobson
Dennis Dobson
Jeff Smith
Eric Brant

Pre-Investigation:

Environmental background readings were taken during this time with nothing significant to note. A discussion with both the male and the female was done during this time to get a better understanding of what they had been experiencing.

Full – Investigation:

Ion Counts:

No significant ion counts either +/- were recorded in the basement, kitchen, living room, dining room, or in the toy room. High concentrations of positive ions have been associated with irritability and negative moods while negative ions have the opposite effect (Charry and Hawkinshire, 1981).

Investigator Personal Experiences:

No personal experiences were noted by any of the investigators present.

Video and Photos:

No anomalies were noted in any of the photographs taken. Video was not recorded.

EVP Sessions:

No EVP Sessions were recorded.

DEAD Data:

There were no changes in any of the environmental data

collected with the DEAD system that correlated with any personal experiences. However, four high EMF spikes were noted in the living room area during one part of the evening.

The readings were noted as:

Time	Axis Affected	Sum Reading
19:53:19	(Y) 296.9	296.9 mG
19:53:53	(Y) 281.7	282 mG
19:54:02	(Y) 259.3	259.3 mG
19:54:11	(Y) 163.5	165.1 mG

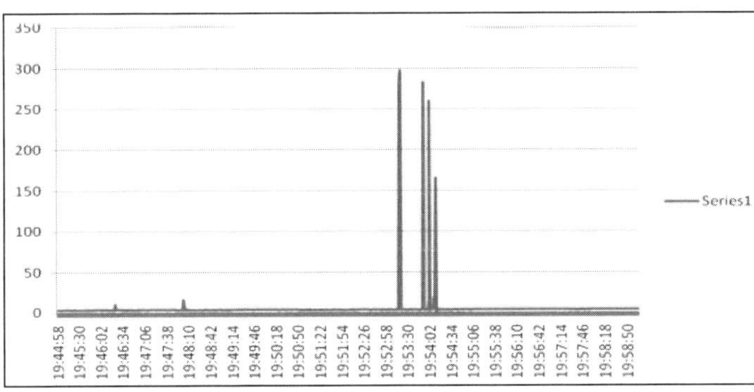

Graph of four high EMF spikes captured in the living room.

Variability in the electro and natural magnetic fields was seen throughout the locations where the client reported paranormal activity. EMF amplitude and frequency changes have been noted in other investigations of "haunted" locations. Other research has implicated that low frequencies are important for triggering neurophysiological shifts and invoking experiences in individuals. Naturally produced geomagnetic fields have also been implicated in reports of anomalous activity. In addition, magnetic field variability in the 11 to 15nT range has been detected in locations where people have reported paranormal activity. Even though the pulses are created from the 60Hz field, it could be detected by the brain as a change in the static field. Even though AC fields are not complex magnetic fields, they can be complex in the fact that they vary in time and amplitude. Further monitoring of these fields during times when the family reports paranormal experiences is recommended.

QRNG Monitoring:

A Psyleron Quantum Based Random Number Generator (QRNG) was placed in the residence where RSPK experiences were reported. It was set up according to the specifications provided in the instruction manual. It ran at a rate of 200 bits per second. The provided FieldREG software was used to collect, graph and export the data.

From what the female homeowner had told me about what she had been experiencing, I decided to do some testing on this subject. During one part of the evening, I wanted to see if the female homeowner could consciously influence the Psyleron Quantum Based Random Number Generator (QRNG).

We began running the QRNG in the Kitchen at a table while viewing the monitor. I asked her to focus on altering the data points on the screen. She did for awhile then began getting very tired. She began to lose focus and looked very flushed. I then asked her to stop focusing on the graph and we shut the screen off but left the QRNG running as we began to talk about generals. The following graph is what was captured during that session. No other data was recorded at that time.

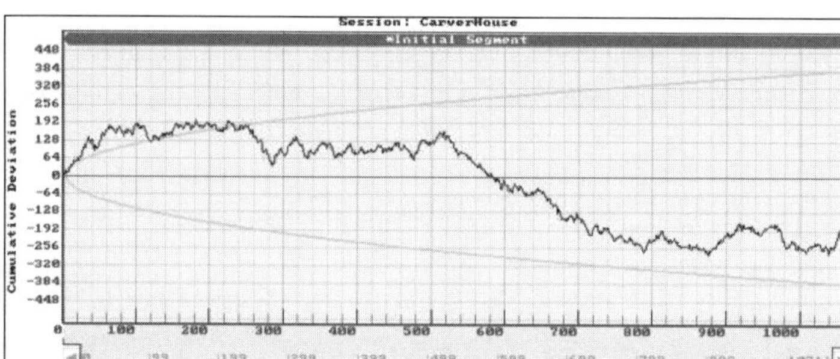

Graph of female influencing the Quantum Random Number Generator in the kitchen.

During the time we had gotten the high EMF spikes on the Dead System, we were running the QRNG as well and the following graph represents the data chart being influenced at the time.

Graph of the Quantum Random Number Generator being influenced by the high EMF spikes.

Conclusion:

A paranormal causation for the reported activity is thought to be Psychokinesis (PK) by the Investigators of the SWPRG. Psychokinesis (PK) is the hypothesized ability of the mind to influence physical objects and processes. It is commonly referred to as mind-over-matter. PK can be divided into two categories depending on the size of effect. Micro-PK involves effects that occur on a very small scale down to the microscopic and/or atomic level where results are observed with the aid of computers, statistical analysis, and other advanced equipment. Macro-PK occurs on a large scale and includes such things as: psychic healing and psychic surgery; materialization and dematerialization of objects; teleportation; the imprinting of images on film or video; and the imprinting of sounds and voices on tapes or other recording devices.

Poltergeist activity, which was more appropriately termed by William Roll as Recurrent Spontaneous Psychokinesis (R.S.P.K.), is thought to be a form of PK that is centered around and produced by a living person called the agent. The agent that activity is centered around is sometimes under stress and the RSPK is the result of the subconscious mind releasing the stress via PK. Despite the reported macro-PK events reported during poltergeist outbreaks, the agents are not generally able to produce PK effects when tested in the laboratory. The client is urged to continue to keep a journal of the experiences they have and stay in touch with the SWPRG.

References:

Irwin & Watt. *An Introduction to Parapsychology*. Jefferson, NC. McFarland and Company, Inc. (2007)

Roll, William. Some psychical and psychological aspects of a series of poltergeist phenomena. *Journal of the American Society for Psychical Research*. 62, 263-308. (1968)

Roll, William. *Poltergeists*. (1977)

Wolman (Ed.). *Handbook of Parapsychology*. New York, NY. VonNostrand Reinhold.

Bender. *Modern Poltergeist Research*. (1974)

Belof (Ed.). In *New Directions in Parapsychology*. London. Elek Science.

Schumacher, David *PSI Journal of Investigative Psychical Research* (Vol 5. Number 1.) Non-Random Output of a Random Number Generator During an Apparent Poltergeist/RSPK Experience: A Case Study (2009)

The following was an email sent from the home owners regarding the report on: Wednesday, October 14, 2009 9:39 AM

Hello Jennifer,

After reading and re-reading your report, and studying some subjects on the internet, I have some questions. I was too stunned on Sunday to think of any then.

1. Why didn't you test my husband on the computer too? What was so convincing in my test that you didn't think it necessary to test him? As we told you Sunday, Many times I suspected he was the person who was responsible for the missing objects and accused him of it. He, as usual, only laughed and denied it.

Over the 6-1/2 year period involved, he never initiated a conversation regarding the problem of missing items, he would only laugh when I would inform him of another item missing.

There are a couple of other reasons why I can be suspicious of him. They are too personal to reveal, yet, but I can see why he would be glad if I was to move out which I have threatened to do several times.

2. Jeff Smith is listed as a member of your investigation team. I don't find him listed in your web site. What was his part in the investigations here? Also, who was the gentleman with you on Sunday, was he Eric Brandt? Was he here for the Jan. 24 investigation?

3. Although I would be very happy to be able to completely disregard any possibility of having a haunted house by anyone or anything, I don't see anything in your report that actually shows me where it has been disregarded as a possible source of our missing items and strange incidents.

4. Even if I believe that it was possible for me to use this "power" to commit these acts, can you tell me why I never "removed or "stole" any items belonging to my husband? I can't figure out --- if I have this "power" I'm sure I would have used it long ago to pack up myself and my belongings and move out of this house. That has been my wish for quite some time now.

I will continue to study about this so-called power of mine, but I will absolutely need a lot more PROOF that it exists and that I am responsible for every strange incident in the last 6-1/2 years.

Jennifer's reply to the home owners questions on: Friday, October 16, 2009 5:16 PM

Thank you for your questions and I will answer them to the best of my ability.

Here are a few things to consider in regards to testing:

1. Your husband was in the house when some of the testing was done so he could have influenced it as well.

These types of tests/experiments are only exploratory in nature. They are NOT diagnostic. In addition, a review of the published literature in the field would indicate that R.S.P.K. (Recurrent Spontaneous Psychokinesis) agents perform poorly when asked to influence devices to prove their mind-over-matter ability. One test one time will not definitively prove or disprove anything.

2. Jeff Smith was an investigator and his role was to collect and record data and report it to the Lead Investigator, which was me. All information from the investigation team was compiled and included in the report. Jeff voluntarily left the group due to personal reasons.

3. Dave Schumacher was the person who came with me on Sunday. He was there for the January 24th investigation. Dave

was the Science & Technology Advisor for the SWPRG at the time we conducted your investigation. Dave has been involved in paranormal research and investigation for over 15 years. He holds an advanced degree in biology. He also has taken a considerable amount coursework in psychology and chemistry. He has taken an advanced university parapsychology course, co-authored a book with me, taught paranormal education classes at various colleges and published scientific papers in peer- reviewed journals.

4. In regards to the report not having anything in it to completely rule out the possibility of a haunted house (haunted by anyone or anything as you stated in your email)......There is no way to prove a negative. It is not acceptable to try to prove a negative in scientific and other types of investigations. The acceptable method is to collect information, gather evidence, and data and form a hypothesis (of which I stated in the report that this was a hypothesis) based on the best-available information. If we consider that the activity is paranormal in nature and not due to fraud and/or misinterpretation, then based on the information we currently have, the activity you reported best fits with the RSPK/Poltergeist activity. This is based on the information you told us and data collected during the investigation. RSPK/Poltergeist activity is centered around and produced by a living person called the agent; that person is usually under some sort of stress; object movement is common; and object disappearance and reappearance has been reported. In addition, the phenomenon itself is centered on objects or areas that are symbolic of the cause of stress. This focusing can occur in three possible ways: "area"-focused; "object"-focused or "individual object"-focused. This also addresses some of the issues in point #4 in your e-mail. There may very well be a reason as to why only your items are affected but that would involve a much deeper understanding of the situation and really studying the psychology, thoughts, and emotions involved with your situation and your relationship with your husband.

We are not psychologists or therapists. Therefore, we would strongly encourage you to seek out a professional to work with you on whatever issues you have with your husband. We can't stress this enough since many times in your e-mail you stated and alluded to issues you have with him.

Finally, I can appreciate your wanting to read more about RSPK to learn more about it. I would recommend that you visit some of these more reputable websites:

American Society for Psychical Research
http://www.aspr.com

Parapsychological Association
http://www.parapsych.org/index.html

Society for Psychical Research
http://www.spr.ac.uk

Public Parapsychology
http://publicparapsychology.blogspot.com

You may also find these books informative:

Handbook of Parapsychology, edited by Benjamin Wolman

An Introduction to Parapsychology, Harvey J. Irwin and Caroline A. Watt

Hauntings and Poltergeists: A Multidisciplinary Perspective, edited by James Houran and Rense Lange.

I hope this information is useful.

The final communication: Saturday, October 18, 2009 10:50 AM

Lauer received a telephone call from the daughter of the home owner. She expressed a great concern over the SWPRG's hypothesized conclusion of this case being RSPK (Recurrent Spontaneous Psychokinesis).

The woman told Jennifer her mother called her and was very upset by what was told to her by the SWPRG during the reveal process. She asked to see a copy of the report that was given to the home owners.

Lauer then sent the daughter a copy of the report and explained what it all meant. The daughter then asked why Jennifer didn't just tell the home owner that the house was haunted by the ghost of her husbands ex-wife and be done with it. That is what her mother wanted to hear.

Lauer proceeded to explain to the daughter that the SWPRG doesn't just tell people what they want to hear. They are in it for the REAL research and documentation of cases.

The woman stated that the female home owner needed to know that it was the ghost of her husbands ex-wife who was creating all of the issues between them. The female home owner was not happy in the house and needed a reason to move out.

Lauer then told the daughter to strongly encourage the home owners to seek out a professional to work with them to help them deal with whatever issues they have between them. There was definitely more personal issues going on than what was told to the researchers during the interviewing process.

In Summation...

Sometimes it's better to step away from a situation, especially one that could be harmful to the psyche of the people involved, then proceed and create an even worse situation. Especially when it involves personal and family relationships.

Janesville Haunted Mansion.

From: Home owners requested to remain anonymous

The following is a recap of the activity the home owners have been experiencing with the house since they purchased it in 2002.

The first year I moved in not a lot happened. Much of the things experienced could have simply been to the new house 'syndrome' or kids with over active imaginations. One of the first things that happened was my son said that he was laying in bed and the rocking chair in the room started to rock back and forth and then a book floated in the air. When he told me about it I thought it was just a hypnagogic hallucination. This would of course be the most reasonable explanation since the house is very old and it would be very reasonable that the kids would be scared, think it might be haunted and let their imagination get a little wild.

Halloween was fast approaching and the creepy house continued to play on the boys. Both of my sons refused to go up stairs by themselves. They never really gave a reason for it besides saying it was creepy up there. What kid wouldn't think a big old house is creepy when it is dark and they are alone upstairs? I continued to assure them that everything was fine and there was no reason to be scared.

As Halloween approached something new began to happen. Starting in late October the front doorbell would ring. I would go to see who was there but no one was ever there. This happened two or three times a week. After awhile I thought it was just some kids in the neighborhood goofing around so I no longer answered the doorbell unless it rang twice and/or the dogs indicated that someone was at the door. I also replaced the doorbell just to make sure it wasn't a mechanical or electrical issue. The doorbell continued to ring even after I changed it. This continued on until the end of December.

Nothing else happened after the doorbell stopped ringing. Well, at least until next October. In October of the second year I lived here the doorbell did not ring but there was knocking at the front door! It sounded like someone opened the storm door and was pounding on the front wooden door. I would go and see who was at the door but just like when the doorbell rang, there was no one there. This happened two or three times a week and I never saw anyone at the door or running away from the door. There was even a time when a few inches of snow had just fallen and I heard the knocking at the front door and I thought for sure I would see footprints in the snow if someone had knocked on the door and ran away. When I went to answer the door there was of course no one there and there were no footprints in the snow!

It is very interesting in that there are two doors at the front entrance. There is the main door, which is the original wooden door to the house and there is another door just to the left of the main door. The door to the left was put in as a second entrance when the house was split into a duplex (split left and right) about 30 years or so ago. When the house was converted back into a single family home the second door was sealed shut and has not been used since. The weird thing is that the knocking only occurred on the big wooden door that is original to the house! There was never any knocking on that second newer door! The knocking on the front door happened on and off from October to December. Once December came and went the knocking at the front door went with it.

However, the October to November time period would soon return and along with it the increasingly weird activity in the house.

The third October I lived here came and so did another series of interesting events. There was no knocking on the front door this year. Instead, there was knocking on the inside walls on the first floor of the house! One memorable event was a night I was sitting in the family room off of the kitchen while the kids were watching TV. All of a sudden there were three loud bangs on the inside wall on the inside wall between the family room and the men's parlor. I was wondering what the hell that was and I started to look around. I walked into the men's parlor to see if I can determine where the knocking came from. As I entered the room and asked out loud, 'what the hell was that?' Whatever it was responded with three very loud bangs on the wall between the men's parlor and the family room. Not only could I hear the loud knocks but I could feel the vibrations. It seemed like whatever it was responded when I asked the question! The knocking and pounding continued until the end of December.

The fourth year in the house proved to be even more interesting. The knocking on the inside walls started to happen throughout the year. I also noticed that the door to the third floor stairs would be found to have opened by itself. This door was just outside of the second floor bedroom with the fireplace. I would close the door just to find it open again a few days later. It started doing it so frequently that I thought it was the kids doing it. They denied ever opening that door. They were scared to go up to the second floor themselves and certainly were not going to venture up to the even creepier third floor!

Even though the kids assured me they were not opening the door I had to make sure they weren't trying to play a trick on me. So, I purchased some of that invisible powder that only shows up under UV light. I coated the doorknob on both sides as well as the floor and stairs on both sides. A few days later the door was open again. I gathered up everyone in the house and checked their hands with the UV light. No one had any of the powder on them. I then went upstairs and checked the door, floor and stairs. To my surprise there were no fingerprints, handprints or footprints. The door opening by itself would remain a mystery.

A few other strange things started to happen on and off during the year. My mother-in-law was staying with us for a bit and a bunch of her jewelry went missing. About six months later she got up one morning, got dressed, made the bed and went downstairs. She then returned to the bedroom about five minutes later and saw all of her missing jewelry in the middle of the bed! This was the bedroom with the fireplace on the second right by the door to the third floor that would open by its self.

There were also numerous times when a toy or some other item would go missing and then just show up in a place where I had just been looking a few minutes earlier. One of the more unnerving events happened when my daughter was six months old. I had just put her to bed in her crib in her room, turned on the baby monitor and then went to my bedroom. After about ten minutes, on the baby monitor, I heard what sounded like something very heavy slide across the floor. I thought "what the hell was that?' I got up and went into my daughter's room and what I saw amazed me...her large 150 pound crib had moved about four feet off of the wall! She was fast asleep! This was amazing but very scary! Making noises, hiding things and opening doors was one thing but when it affects my kids then that is going to far. I put a motion detection camera in that room. If the crib moved again I wanted to be able to capture it! I left the camera in the room for a few days. The bed did not move but the camera did capture some movement. When I reviewed the images captured it looked like there was a very bright flash of light that happened right behind the crib. I checked the weather and there was no thunder or lightening that day. I also made sure that headlights from cars were not the cause. I watched the cars come up the street and then turn the corner and there was no indication that this was a plausible explanation.

I needed to figure out what was going on and that is why I have decided to tell the SWPRG in detail what has been going on. I also think that an ongoing in depth investigation is needed at this point in order to better determine what type of activity might be happening in this house.

Another interesting event happened during the summer when my son was having a birthday party. Everyone was inside and getting ready to open birthday presents. I went outside for a bit and ended up talking to the neighbor. As I was talking to him I saw a small blond haired boy with a yellow shirt and long blue shorts (like knickers) who was about four years old go running around the corner of the house towards the backyard. It looked like he ran between the fence and the lilac bush. I told the neighbor that I had to go cause one of the kids had escaped. I ran over to the backyard and looked all over. The gates were closed and no one was in the yard. I was somewhat confused at this point because I knew I saw someone run into the backyard! I went in the house and asked if one of the kids had gone outside. Everyone said no and all the kids were in the house. This was the first and only time I thought I had perhaps seen an apparition. It was very weird! When I saw the boy the he was in the center of my vision and was very clear. However, the edges seemed fuzzy.

Various people also reported hearing a little girls voice say "mom" and "mommy." Many times people would hear this girls voice and would go looking for the source but never found anything. Then there are the footsteps. Numerous times I would hear footsteps walking across the second floor when I was in the family room and men's parlor. The second floor hallways were carpeted but it always sounded like someone walking on a hardwood floor. The last thing that I can think of at the moment is something that has been happening somewhat frequently in the balcony suite. The bed in that room had moved about a foot or two off of the wall.

I think it would be a great idea to have an ongoing investigation in order to understand what is happening here.

There has been several investigations conducted on this residence. The following are just a few of those reports.

Investigation Report
September 18, 2010

Design: Make all charts that follow larger to fit page space as needed. Enhance.

Journal Entries
From Investigators at the Scene:

9:30 PM	Someone reported seeing a round black shadow go down the hall from Emma's room.
9:35 PM	Asked door to third floor to close and it did.
10:30 PM	Person reported two scratches on their back. Happened in Balcony Suite.
12:13 AM	Noise heard on third floor.
12:21 AM	Someone reported seeing a shadow move on the third floor.
12:26 AM	Loud metallic pop heard on the third floor.
1:45 AM	Heard door slam while sitting in third floor office.
1:45 to 2:00 AM	Heard shuffling sounds on third floor.
2:00 AM	Trifield EMF at 0 then maxed out at 100 at base of stairway by big screen TV. Alarm went off steady at light switch. Approximately at the same time as a 11mG spike in the EMF.
2:20 AM	Heard several footsteps and knocks overhead while in the Widow's Suite. Sometime after that, but before 2:30 AM, we heard a loud cough or throat clearing. Asked all on three floors and no one heard or made similar noise. Approximately the same time there was a 22cpm spike in the radiation.
3:18 AM	Cabinet doors in bathroom in Widow's Suite were open. Approximately at the same time as a 3mG spike in the EMF.

Summary:

Overall all it was a very active night. The door to the third floor closed when an investigator asked it to close, many different sounds were heard, and an EVP was captured. This is also the first time the QRNG achieved and maintained significance in the balcony suite.

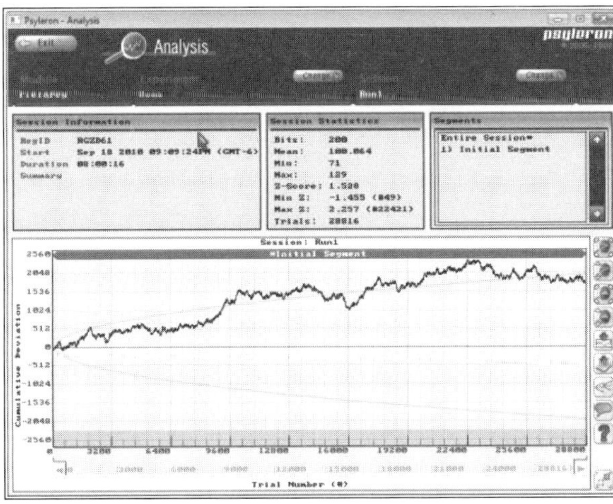

Graph of the Quantum Random Number Generator achieving and maintaining significance in the balcony suite.

Investigation Report:
October 2, 2010

Journal Entries From Investigators at the Scene:

Unknown Time	In the women's parlor, footsteps were heard. They were quick and light and came from above.
10:15 PM	Two people entered Balcony Suite. Goofing around – waiting for the group, and at the same time loudly heard "MOM" in a silly voice to the right side of the fireplace.
12AM	In Balcony Suite, a thud was heard and scratching noise heard near closet.

Little after midnight	We were on the third floor in the office. We took a Maglite twist flashlight (mini), set it on the desk and asked for it to be turned on, and it came on. We asked for it to turn off and it went off. Not once, not twice, but four times, and Jen was witness to the fourth time. After the first time, I turned on my digital camera to video and was able to document the flashlight going on and off two times. We were amazed!
12:30 AM	Door to third floor opens. Check DVR. See analysis/explanation below.
2AM	Several of us were in the Balcony Suite. A flashlight came on by itself by request. A huge temperature drop all the way down to 24 degrees was seen on the combo Temp/EMF meter. Three people saw the readings. The temp went back up quickly to 71 degrees after about five seconds.
2:26 AM	Christine and Joe were standing at door heading up to third floor (near private room) and heard a child's voice say "mommy."
4 to 5:30 AM	Christine and Joe. Had many episodes during this time in the Widow's Suite – banging and noise that sounded like something was being dragged across the floor above them (3rd floor). Also heard what sounded like someone whispering out in the hall (will see if I captured it on my digital recorder).
5:00am	Christine and Joe were in Widows Suite. Many pounding noises from the third floor were heard.
5:00am	Betty. In Men's Parlor. Felt tingling sensation up and down back like someone touching me. Back was on couch.

Video/Pictures:

A video of a flashlight turning on and off by itself was captured by overnight investigators Steve and Sherri.

Someone noted that the door to the third floor opened by itself at 12:30 AM. After reviewing the DVR video, a person was seen opening the door and pushing it with their hand while they were on the inside of the door on the first step. About a minute later, someone comes down the stairs and then a second person falls in behind them from the right side of the stairway on the first step. Therefore, it is concluded that the door did not open by itself in this instance.

Summary:

Overall, it was again another active night. A couple of people reported a variety of different experiences. Sounds of thuds, pounding, things being dragged across the floor and whispering were heard. On two occasions, people either heard "mom" or "mommy" being called out by a little girl. Also, there were four instances when a Maglite flashlight turned on and off by itself when asked to do so. Finally, a 48 degree temperature drop was noted on a handheld thermometer.

Investigation Report
October 9, 2010

Journal Entries From Investigators at the Scene:

11:08 PM	Second floor hallway between Balcony Suite and Emma's Room, heard a growl, got a 4.99mG EMF spike and person on bed in balcony suite reported a nudge or bump against the bed.
1:00 AM	Was sitting in balcony suite, when hostess came up, and asked if we made whimpering noises, we replied no... Checked random number generator. It was spiked, 30min later another member asked upon entering the room, if we pounded on floor. We didn't. Number generator was spiking again.

1:28 AM	Men's parlor – bump, bump above without movement on monitor from balcony suite.
2:52 AM	On couch in men's parlor, old fashioned piano music seemed to come from below and possible children humming.
Unknown times	Initial sweep on 3rd floor – office door had 5.2mG EMF spike and 1.3mG EMF spike. Very brief. Second sweep – second floor balcony suite closet doorway EMF spike 1.8mG and geiger counter spike of 1.0. top of stairs EMF 1.45mG. bottom of stairs EMF 17mG spike and middle of stairs EMF spike 4.57-5.00mG.

Video/Pictures:

Nothing of interest was found in any of the videos or pictures.

Summary:

Overall, it was a good investigation. Not as many personal experiences as the prior two investigations but there was still enough to keep it interesting. The number of EMF "spikes" both on the handheld and data-logging equipment was interesting and some correlated with personal experiences. The QRNG achieved and maintained significance in the opposite direction. This is the opposite direction compared to what happen with the QRNG during the September 18th, 2010 investigation.

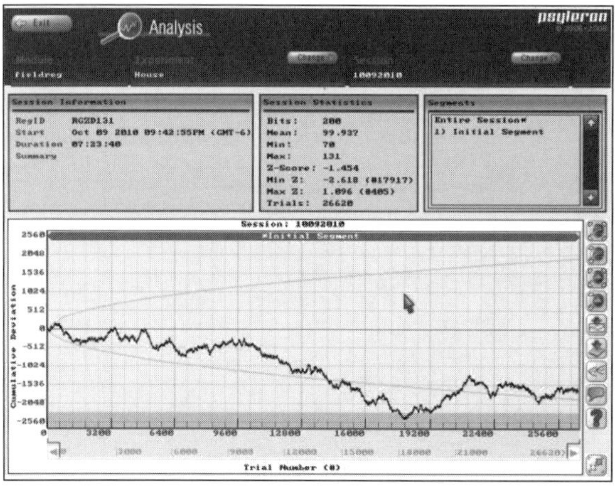

Graph of the Quantum Random Number Generator achieving and maintaining significance in the opposite direction.

Investigator Comments:

In 2009, this mansion went up for sale and the owners moved out. We talked to them about taking over the mortgage payments and moving in to use it as an ongoing paranormal research lab. The owners agreed, and in April 2010, we moved in. We have been working in the paranormal field for over 20 years and we can honestly say that we have had more experiences living in this mansion over the past year than anywhere else we have ever investigated.

Investigation Report
October 15, 2010

Journal Entries
From Investigators at the Scene

11:30 PM	I had my batteries drained in both my camera and digital recorder.
12:30 AM	In Emma's room sitting on floor. Felt pressure on upper thigh.
1AM	In quiet time, we were in Emma's room. I felt something running hands thru the left side of my hair.
2AM	As a group, we were by the stairs at the men's lounge. Many heard a young girl making "whooohoo" sounds and I caught it on my recorder. Also, just after that, I caught a foreign voice on my recorder.
3:30 AM	Sitting in men's parlor, the trunk thumped enough to move the candy dish.
4AM	Emma's room – I felt like fingers running up my lower left leg. I asked them if it was them touching my leg and told them it was ok. Then it felt like my lower left leg got squeezed then it was gone.

4:50 AM	Joe was standing in the hall by private rooms, after hearing what sounded like a chair being rolled around from the third floor. While standing by the door to the third floor, outside of the private rooms, he heard a growl. He ran back to the widow's room.
5:10 AM	Standing in hallway 2nd floor near entrance to 3rd floor and Dave's room. Felt something blow in my ear and made my hair move. Turned flashlight on and looked upstairs to 3rd floor and behind door. No one was there.
5:15 AM	In Women's parlor. Two screws missing from my camera. Small piece from end of camera taken off, lying under couch but camera still on table.
5:15 AM	Heard a growl-like sound and a "whoo" sound. All in Balcony Suite. Also heard sound like someone was rubbing up against the wall 3 times as well as some banging.

Video/Pictures:

Nothing of interest was found in any of the video recordings or pictures.

Summary:

It was a good investigation. Many personal experiences were reported throughout the night. There were a few "spikes" in the EMF and radiation, but they did not correlate with any personal experiences.

The following is an email from a person who spent some time at the mansion and wanted to tell her story.

My Experiences at the Mansion

Thursday, December 30, 2010 10:04 AM
From: Sarah, Beloit, WI

On September 28th 2010 I was watching the haunted mansions live webcam and there was another person in there watching with me as well. We were just sitting and chatting and at about 10:30 p.m. I noticed something that seemed to be blocking out the light on the brown door that tends to open and close on its own. I went full screen and seen a figure standing there next to the brown door, and it was also blocking out the light on part of the bathroom door frame which is at the end of the hall. It was the first time I've ever seen anything like that on the webcam and I've been watching it since they first started with the live webcam. I pointed it out to the others in the chat room that night. We could actually make out the arms and the head which seemed to be moving, and the long hair. I took some pictures with my cell phone and sent them to Jen and Dave so they could have a look at them. It seems that the figure is about 4 feet tall or so as it comes up to about the same height as the light switch in the balcony suite. The picture is now used in part of their presentation about the haunted mansion.

That is only one of my experiences. I have had some personal experiences during the overnight investigations offered at the haunted mansion. I have been growled at almost everytime I have been there, normally on the second floor. One time I came over before a haunted history tour to walk around the house and take some pictures before everyone else came over. I went up to the third floor and took some pictures in the study room. Up above the windows in that room there is a metal sign that says SWPRG on it. As I was walking out of the room and into the hallway I heard what sounded like something ringing, so I went back into the room to check it out. I noticed that the sign was rattling. It was not windy out that day. I could not feel any type of vibration around or behind the sign. During the next overnight I went up to the third floor to do an evp session. I asked during that session "are you the one who made that sign rattle?" And when I listened back to my recorder later on I heard a reply to my answer, It sounded as if someone was saying "HmmmHmmm" as in a yes. So after the next overnight was over I went up there again to try to figure out a natural explanation. I pounded on the wall around it, jumped up and down on the floor, walked back and fourth in the room, even went and turned on the dryer, and I could not duplicate it. The only way I was able to get it to do it again was to actually push on the sign itself.

In October I was there for one of the weekends that they had overnights on Friday and Saturday night and then that Sunday there was a meeting at the mansion. Well seeing that I had been up for pretty much 48 hours Jen and Dave let me stay there and get some sleep before the meeting and they didn't want me driving home so tired. They put me up in the widows room on the second floor. I got all situated and laid down on the bed. There is also a private bathroom in this room. As I was laying there I heard a man's raspy voice say very clearly "HEYYYY HEYYYYY HEYYYYYY!". I really wish I had my recorder running at the time! I am wondering if this is the same man who seems to be growling at people. The growl to me sounds more like a frustrated person. I have also been at the mansion during overnights and we clearly heard a little girls voice saying what sounds like "yoohoo" and that happened two nights in a row. In the hallway that leads to the balcony suite I always get a feeling as though I'm being watched. Its not a bad feeling, just that feeling you get when you are being watched.

We also had some interesting responses with a flashlight one time at an overnight. My brother and his girlfriend and their friend joined me for one of the overnights and we took a flashlight up to the rooms with us. In almost every room something turned the flash light on, on command. My brother also got some interesting pictures that night as well. There have also been overnights that I've been to where seemingly nothing happens and it's a pretty uneventful night. You never know when something will happen and things have happened at all times during the day and night. We've seen the door open and close on its own in the morning, and seen it close at night. I was also watching the webcam one night and heard a very loud slam and then the brown door closed halfway. I sent Jen a text message and they said they weren't home at the time, but they would be home soon to check it out. They got home and went and checked it out. At first I thought it was the bathroom door that had slammed shut but apparently that was locked but Dave said that Emma's room door was shut. It almost seemed as whatever it was slammed Emma's door and then ran down the hallway and up the stairs closing the brown door halfway as it was running past, and it happened very quickly. We hear a lot of stuff on the webcam. Sometimes you can hear what sounds like people having a conversation when no one is in the house, footsteps, banging, clanging noises, and we even heard the growl on the webcam once and it sounded like it was right up to the mic. I've also captured these type of noises on my recorder during the overnights but didn't hear it at the time.

Chapter Eight

Why You So Crazy?

This chapter focuses on the Author's themselves and their personal stories and inspiration behind what drives them to do what they do — investigate the paranormal!

Our Inspiration

Jennifer Lauer

When I was young, I would try to soak up all the information I could about new paranormal cases I would hear about. One case that really peaked my interest in the paranormal growing up was known as, "The Smurl Haunting." The Smurl home of West Pittston, Pennsylvania, was the scene of a very controversial haunting from 1985 to 1987. The case received a huge amount of media attention and was chronicled in a book and portrayed in a movie both named, *The Haunted*. This case was investigated by demonologists, Ed and Lorraine Warren but was later investigated by The Committee for the Scientific Investigation of Claims of the Paranormal (CSICOP). Their investigation revealed this case to be a hoax.

Another case that grabbed my attention while growing up was a local one from Horicon, Wisconsin. In 1987, The Tallmann family – Allen and Debbie; two toddlers, and an infant – lived in a small, three-bedroom ranch house on Larrabee Street. They reported several strange phenomena which they tracked back to an old bunk bed that was in the children's bedroom. Many reports consisted of furniture flying around the house, blinds going up and down, blood dripping from the ceiling, lights coming on with the power off, writings on the walls, green lights flashing, an apparition of an old lady, and flames shooting from their garage.

This case also had a huge amount of media coverage. A quote taken from the *Milwaukee Journal Sentinel's* interview with the family on Wednesday, January 27, stated that around the beginning of January 1988, the father said the entity made a threat. The quote: "This thing came right out of the floor. It was gassy and foggy ... It rose up there and that voice came out of there and it said, 'You're dead.' These green eyes appeared right out of this thing, and then I saw flames and it was gone."

In January 1988, I was 19 years old and I remember driving up to Horicon with a friend to try and find the "Haunted House." My friend and I even went to the local library to try and find any possible information on this house...but we failed. This case was never disproved and to this day, remains one of Wisconsin's most famous mysterious paranormal cases.

The Ghost Hunter's Guidebook by author Troy Taylor was one of the first books that gave me the inspiration to look at this as more than just a hobby. Besides being an author of over thirty-five books on the paranormal, Troy Taylor is also the President of the American Ghost Society, a nationally known Paranormal Group. The AGS holds an annual conference every year, which I have attended many times.

Dave Schumacher

In 1984, I remember my parents showing me an incredible picture in the local newspaper. The picture, taken by Fred Shannon of the Columbus, Ohio, *Dispatch*, showed Tina Resch sitting on a chair with a telephone in mid-air flying across her body. The story below the picture described lights going on and off by themselves, clocks stopping and starting, cabinet doors opening and closing and a variety of objects flying about the home. The famous parapsychologist Dr. William Roll investigated the case. In addition to Dr. Roll, members from the Committee for the Scientific Investigation of Claims of the Paranormal (CSICOP) took a more skeptical approach to the case. James "Amazing" Randi and two scientists from Case Western University were also on hand to get to the bottom of the strange happenings. Dr. Roll claimed the case to be a true example of poltergeist activity (or Recurrent Spontaneous Psychokinesis, RSPK for you science geeks) while CSICOP and Randi said it was a fraud. There is still no consensus whether this was a genuine case of paranormal activity or a hoax. Either way, it was my first serious exposure to poltergeist phenomena and I began my search for other similar stories.

Like Jennifer, "The Smurl Haunting" case fascinated me. I will never forget reading the book, *The Haunted,* by Robert Curran in my parents' basement (no comments about ghost geeks living in their parent's basement). The story both intrigued and frightened me. Fortunately, my fear quickly gave way for my quest for understanding and knowledge.

A few years later, I discovered the movie, *The Entity*. This 1983 horror film was based on a real case and is one of the most famous cases in paranormal history. The story was extensively covered in *Omni Magazine*, *Fate*, and on the television show *Sightings* in 1992. I was and still am fascinated by this case. In 1974, Carla Moran began her terrifying experience while living in Culver City, California. She experienced a variety of paranormal phenomena including but not limited to: strange smells, electrical malfunctions, cold spots, and object movement. This may seem bad enough... but it got worse. She also reported being repeatedly raped and beaten by the ghost. It was at this point that she began to seek professional help.

Carla approached Dr. Kerry Gaynor and Dr. Barry Taff. Dr. Gaynor and Dr. Taff were parapsychologists who worked with Dr. Thelma Moss from UCLA. Carla explained her terrifying ordeal. Initially, Dr. Gaynor and Dr. Taff considered the whole story rather unbelievable and seriously thought that Carla needed psychological counseling. However, Carla continued to discuss her horrifying situation with the two parapsychologists and eventually they decided to investigate the case.

When Dr. Taff and Dr. Gaynor arrived at Carla's house, what they saw amazed them. They experienced pops of light, cabinet doors opening and closing by themselves and a partial apparition form before their very eyes. Using a Geiger counter, they documented background radiation levels dropping to zero when the phenomena occurred and returning to normal when the activity ceased. This is the first case that I know of where radiation levels were measured and why some paranormal investigators continue to monitor radiation levels. The most impressive thing they saw were arcs of light over Carla's head. The lights first started on the walls but then came off of the wall and kept moving in the air. The researchers captured a picture of the phenomena that clearly shows an arc of light over Carla's head and completely off the wall. This photo appeared in *Popular Photography* and it was the first and last paranormal picture to appear in that magazine.

Carla Moran moved five times to try to escape her otherworldly tormentor. The phenomena that plagued and tormented her diminished slightly with each move. The majority of the activity ceased after about two years. Because the activity followed her, was centered on her, and pretty much stopped after two years, Dr. Taff and Dr. Gaynor and Dr. Moss thought that this might have been a poltergeist case. At this point, I thought there must be something to all of this and it would be worthwhile to explore further. I craved more information. I wanted to know what a poltergeist really was and what parapsychologists really did. Are ghosts real? Is there any proof of life after death? At this exact point I came across a book that would solidify my interest in this area for the rest of my life, *ESP, Hauntings and Poltergeists: A Parapsychologists Handbook* by Loyd Auerbach, published in 1986. This book had it all and a REAL parapsychologist wrote it! It covered the following:

- Apparitions, poltergeists, and hauntings (yes, there is a difference).
- What is a parapsychologist?
- What is psi?
- What is extrasensory perception (ESP)?
- Out-of-body experiences.
- Near death experiences.
- Possible natural explanations for subjective paranormal experiences.
- The impact of paranormal movies on the public's perception of the phenomenon. *Real*-life cases.
- How the Amityville Horror was nothing more than wild fiction (what a bummer).
- How to be a paranormal investigator.
- What questions to ask and why.

I think I have read this book at least five times. It gave me my first serious information on the paranormal and how to investigate it. I still refer to it often and I strongly encourage all would-be ghost hunters and paranormal investigators to read this book.

Personal Experiences
What Keeps Us Going?

According to a recent Gallop Poll, 3 out of 4 Americans hold some paranormal belief. Americans are known to believe in extrasensory perception (ESP), ghosts, haunted houses, communicating with the dead, mental telepathy, clairvoyance, astrology, witches, reincarnation, and channeling. This must be pretty accurate, because if it wasn't, we wouldn't be called to do investigations. We have both experienced paranormal phenomena to a certain level that we cannot explain. Some of these experiences were during paranormal investigations and some were not...but either way, they have been the experiences that keep us going. Our experiences are what drives us to keep pursuing this field and to make sense out of it all.

Jennifer Lauer

I have had many strange occurrences happen to me that I cannot explain away fully. Looking back, I have found one specific component that has remained the same throughout: The majority have all been audible experiences.

A Whisper

Before I ever organized the SWPRG, I had an experience that still to this day I can't explain. I was 21 years old and had just moved into the house that my grandparents owned while I was growing up. My grandfather, Arthur, died in the front room of a heart attack in 1977, while my 10 year-old brother, John, watched. My bedroom was the same one my grandparents shared for their entire married life. I always loved this room. It was right in the front of the house and had lots of windows and was bright and cheery most of the time. Even at night, the lights from the outside would shine in and make it feel as if it were a warm, cozy, inviting room...until one night.

I walked into the house around 11:30 PM after my second-shift job. Everyone in the house was already asleep. I sat down in the living room and began watching television for a couple of hours before deciding to head off to bed around 1AM. That night seemed no different than any other night, until I shut off all the lights, got into bed, and started to settle in. Within a few minutes I could hear a quick whispery voice talking. I could definitely hear it, but I couldn't understand what it was saying. I not only heard it, but I could feel the warm breath on my ear as it talked. I was suddenly frozen in my bed of fear, so I quickly grabbed my pillow and pulled the ends up around my head and covered my ears. Within seconds, I heard it again. I felt the breath on my ear just like before, but this time it was as if the pillow wasn't even there. This experience shocked me so much that I never mentioned this to anyone else in the house.

Three months later, my mother, who lived in the house as well, told me of a strange experience she had the previous night. She proceeded to tell me of the exact same events that had happened to me three months earlier. At that point, I confided in her that it had happened to me as well. To this day, I still cannot explain the exact same experience my mother and I both had in that house. My mother still lives in that house today, but has never experienced that again. She has had other types of experiences in the house though, but on a much more subtle level.

Go Away!

Another experience that stands out clearly in my mind happened during the investigation of the Spaulding House Antique Shop in Janesville, Wisconsin. The Spaulding house property is one of Janesville's oldest reported haunted locations, not to mention the location of the first murder ever recorded in Rock County. Joseph and Lydia Spaulding built the house in 1870. In 1877, Joseph Spaulding actually died in the house, and although Lydia died several years later in another house in downtown Janesville, all of the telltale signs of this haunting lead to Lydia herself. Most of the past employees of this Antique shop and other businesses that have been on this property swear that Lydia Spaulding *is* the ghost that haunts this property.

Our team did a full investigation of the property. It was close to midnight and we had just about exhausted all of our media devices. The owner of the Antique Shop, Tom, and I were standing near the front door about two feet away from each other. There was no one else in the room. Our team was in another room several feet away from us finishing up an EVP session when something amazing happened. As I stated earlier, Tom and I were standing about two feet away from each other in a room only occupied by the two of us, when all of a sudden the disembodied voice of a women came up between the two of us and said, "Go Away!"

We both heard it...plain as day and neither one could explain where this strange voice came from. Was this Lydia? Was she tiring of us and wanted us to leave "her" home? Whatever the reason, this is something that I could not logically or scientifically explain away. Throughout my career as a paranormal investigator, this was the experience that I can't seem to find ANY natural reason for...but of course, the experiences don't stop there.

Is There A Doctor in the House?

Another audio experience that I was honored to have experienced occurred at what used to be a place called Manteno State Hospital, in Manteno, Illinois. This hospital has since been torn down...yet remains the location of one of the most interesting audio experiences I have ever had. Although *most* of my personal experiences have been just that, *my* personal experiences, I was fortunate to capture on video/audio tape one of the rarest paranormal occurrences ever.

My team and I were investigating one of the many buildings that made up this huge hospital. We had our Natural Tri-Field meter sitting on a table on the second floor inside the "Dix" building. The audio was turned up on our meter so that we could hear if something entered its field. While we investigated, we had a video camera taping the table with the Tri-Field meter on it the entire time.

Then it happened! A noticeable dip in the tone of the Tri-Field meter and then the voice of a nurse paging a doctor from a non-existent PA system. Not *only* did we capture it on video, but also our investigators actually heard it as it was happening. Now, let me remind you that this place has been abandoned for close to 20 years, there was absolutely *no* power running to any of these buildings and the walls were literally falling down around us. No PA system existed in any of the buildings. This wasn't just your average everyday EVP; this had every element possible to use it as factual evidence. It was detected with a natural Tri-Field meter, it was captured on video, and three investigators experienced it all at the same time. What better correlation could you have?

Dave Schumacher

My personal paranormal experiences are few and far between. Two of them involved a specific smell and the other was audio. The interesting thing is that other people who were with me also had the experience.

Lilacs

My first experience happened about eight years ago in November while I was attending a work meeting out on the east coast. We had a few free hours to ourselves and I decided to go for a walk with a co-worker through the historic city that we were staying in. As we proceeded down the street, we saw an old church with a cemetery and thought it would be interesting to walk through the old graveyard. About halfway through the cemetery, I smelled fresh lilacs for about two minutes in a small, confined area. The person I was with smelled it as well. We continued to walk and came back to the same spot about five minutes later to see if we could find the source of the lilacs. However, the smell was gone. We could not find any natural source for the smell. No flowers on any graves, no windows open in the church, and it was about 20 degrees out with no leaves on the trees and certainly no flowers blooming anywhere.

My next experience, which would be another smell, would not happen for another seven years.

A Rose By Any Other Name...

In June 2005, I visited the Ohio State Reformatory. The prison opened in 1896 as a self-sufficient facility for the rehabilitation of male offenders by hard work and education. There were 6 tiers, 12 ranges with 600 cells. It covered an enormous 250,000 square feet. The 6-tier east cellblock is the world's tallest freestanding steel cellblock. The prison hit its highest attendance in 1955 with 5,235 prisoners. However, with changing times and new facilities being built, the inmate population began its eventual decline and most of the prisoners were gone by 1972. In 1983, the building was added to the National Register of Historic Places and completely closed as a functional facility in 1984. The Ohio State Reformatory has been seen in movies such as *The Shawshank Redemption*, *Tango and Cash*, and *Air Force One*.

So, why is it haunted? Why would it be any more haunted than any other prison? All prisons have pain and suffering. However, the Ohio State Reformatory seems to have had more than its fair share. Twenty-eight men were hanged between the years of 1885 to 1897 in the Annex at the east end of East Hall. The fate of death row inmates would change from hangings to the electric chair. Three hundred and fifteen people died in the electric chair between 1897 to 1963 at Ohio State Reformatory. As if this was not enough death, more people died at the prison, even those with out an official death sentence met their end there. A fire on April 21, 1930, claimed the lives of 322 people. In 1950, the warden's wife was removing a jewelry box from a closet shelf in the on-site warden's quarters when the pistol fell off of the shelf. The shock of the pistol hitting the floor caused it to fire. The warden's wife was fatally wounded. Within another ten years, the warden himself died of a heart attack while working in his office. As one can see, if ever a place would be haunted, this would be the place.

The Ohio State Reformatory offers ghost tours at certain times during the year. The Southern Wisconsin Paranormal Research Group hosted a tour of this phenomenal facility in June 2005. It was about two in the morning when I was walking down a hallway in the warden's quarters with two other people. As we came down the hallway, we all suddenly smelled roses. Now, there is NO reason that we should have smelled roses. This place is old, damp and has an overpowering musty/moldy smell. But the smell was there! We followed the smell, which seemed to be moving down the hallway, until it suddenly disappeared. Just as it was gone, we turned the corner and came upon ten other investigators. I asked if any of them had smelled roses and they all said, "Yes." They had been tracking it for the last thirty minutes or so. We spent the next hour or so investigating that smell. Many times it would come and go and move up and down the hallway and go in and out of various rooms in the warden's quarters. And as before, it would abruptly go away.

Could it have been a sign of the warden's wife? Or was it just because we were all really tired and open to suggestion? Who knows! But it was pretty darn cool. This one is pretty hard for me to explain naturally. I like the fact that we experienced it before we had any idea that the other group of people smelled the same thing. Also, the fact that it moved around the warden's quarters was very interesting!

Footsteps

My most recent experience happened on September 26th, 2005, in Watertown, Wisconsin. The incident involved both Jennifer and I. We had done a full investigation of the home and we were back to go over the findings with the owner. While playing and discussing two EVPs that we had captured during the investigation, I distinctly heard five to six loud footsteps on the second floor. Not only could I hear them, but I could feel the vibrations as well! Jennifer looked at me and said, "Did you hear that?" I said, "Yes" and so did the owner. We bolted upstairs to investigate. There was no one there! We spent some time trying to recreate the situation but were unsuccessful. We went back downstairs and discussed what we had just experienced. The homeowner was very excited and relieved that we had heard that because that was what she was hearing all of the time and now she knew she wasn't crazy!

These are the kinds of experiences that keep us searching for the unknown. They move us, motivate us, and drive us in the direction that keeps us ahead of the pack! Without our experiences, how would we know what to look for?

Ever since childhood, we have pursued the paranormal field as a main interest in both of our lives. Individually, we have been investigating and researching paranormal activity for many years until we met in 2002. Ever since, we have combined our talents and experience investigating paranormal activity together and with the other members of the Southern Wisconsin Paranormal Research Group. We have investigated public and private places all over the United States, from huge abandoned prisons and hospitals to private residences.

As well as investigating the paranormal, we also hold classes on Ghost Hunting and have been the guest speakers for many paranormal-based presentations including historical societies and schools. We have both had experience organizing and maintaining paranormal research groups of our own during our professional careers and continue to train and direct other paranormal investigators to bring their intellectual paranormal knowledge to a higher understanding and to what we have been calling, "The Next Level."